The Politics of Disablement

Critical Texts in Social Work and the Welfare State

General Editor: *Peter Leonard*

Pete Alcock and Phil Harris
Welfare Law and Order

*Ragnhild Banton, Paul Clifford, Stephen Frosh,
Julian Lousada, Joanna Rosenthall*
The Politics of Mental Health

Paul Corrigan and Peter Leonard
Social Work Practice Under Capitalism:
A Marxist Approach

Lena Dominelli and Eileen McLeod
Feminist Social Work

Ian Gough
The Political Economy of the Welfare State

Chris Jones
State Social Work and the Working Class

Paul Joyce, Paul Corrigan, Mike Hayes
Striking Out: Social Work and Trade Unionism, 1970-1985

Peter Leonard
Personality and Ideology: Towards A Materialist
Understanding of the Individual

Chris Phillipson
Capitalism and the Construction of Old Age

Michael Oliver
The Politics of Disablement

FORTHCOMING

Peter Leonard
A Critical History of Social Work Theory

Goran Therborn
Welfare States and Advanced Capitalism

Series Standing Order

If you would like to receive future titles in this series as they are published, you can make use of our standing order facility. To place a standing order please contact your bookseller or, in case of difficulty, write to us at the address below with your name and address and the name of the series. Please state with which title you wish to begin your standing order. (If you live outside the United Kingdom we may not have the rights for your area, in which case we will forward your order to the publisher concerned.)

Customer Services Department, Macmillan Distribution Ltd, Houndmills, Basingstoke, Hampshire, RG21 2XS, England.

The Politics of Disablement

First published 1990 by
THE MACMILLAN PRESS LTD
Houndmills, Basingstoke, Hampshire RG21 2XS
and London
Companies and representatives
throughout the world

ISBN 0–333–43292–4 hardcover
ISBN 0–333–43293–2 paperback

A catalogue record for this book is available
from the British Library.

Reprinted 1991, 1992, 1993, 1994

Printed in Hong Kong

To Joy Melinda

For Eleanor, William, Dan and Jemma,
without whom the book might never have
been finished

'The wind, the wind is blowing
Through the graves the wind is blowing
Freedom soon will come
Then we'll come from the shadows.'

Hy Zaret and Anna Marly, *The Partisan*

Contents

Acknowledgements

Throughout the years, many disabled people have contributed to the development of my thinking about disability; in their writings, in conversations and sometimes in heated arguments. It would be invidious to single any of them out by name but I am grateful to them all.

There are some individuals whose contributions I wish to acknowledge, however. My colleague Gerry Zarb for his continuing interest in the project and, in particular, his contribution to Chapter 8, which is very much a joint effort. Amanda Hoad and Myra Telfer also put up with me and allowed me to bounce my ideas off them, often at the cost of not getting on with their own work.

For giving me both shelter and encouragement I am grateful to Lou Opit and his colleagues John Butler, Mike Calnan, Jan Pahl and Peter Allen. Vic George and Dave Reason also allowed me to share my ideas with them.

There is a real sense in which this book would never have been finished without the assistance of Linda, Jill, Maurice and George.

The now defunct Manpower Services Commission provided me with a wordprocessor which made the task of writing so much easier. However, despite my coming to terms with new technology, the final manuscript was put in order by Cathy Lewington in her usual precise and efficient way.

Finally, I am grateful to the Economic and Social Research Council, not simply because they awarded me a personal research grant to carry out the project, but in so doing, have attempted to place the issue of disability firmly on the academic agenda.

MICHAEL OLIVER

Introduction

The issue of disability and the experiences of disabled people have been given scant consideration in academic circles. Both the issue and the experience have been marginalised and only in the disciplines of medicine and psychology has disability been afforded an important place. Unfortunately this has, itself, been counterproductive because it has resulted in the issue of disability being seen as essentially a medical one and the experience of disability as being contingent upon a variety of psychological adjustment processes. Hence there is an urgent need for other disciplines such as sociology, anthropology, history, politics and social administration to take these matters seriously rather than to merely offer descriptive and atheoretical accounts which leave medical and psychological approaches unchallenged.

In order to counter the medical and psychological dominance in this area, ultimately nothing less than a 'social theory of disability' will be necessary, but such a theory cannot be produced until the various academic disciplines begin to take both the issue of disability and the experiences of disabled people seriously in their own right rather than as marginal to both theoretical developments and empirical work.

In the introduction to a book on the work of the Italian sociologist Antonio Gramsci, Peter Hamilton claims

Like many a sociologist his understanding of the underpinnings of his society was formed through a marginalising experience. (Bocock, 1986, p. 7)

As a disabled sociologist, my own experience of marginalisation has been more from the sociological community than from society at large.

A sociologist having either a personal or a professional interest in disability will not find disability occupies a central or even a marginal place on the sociological agenda. And even where it does appear, sociology has done little except reproduce the medical approach to the issue. In recent years medical sociology has grown faster than most other areas, but even within this sub-division, medical sociologists have been unable to distinguish between illness and disability and have proceeded as if they are the same thing.

A similar situation is found within the sister discipline of social anthropology. The anthropology of health and illness has attracted much attention in recent years but again, anthropologists working in this area have not even questioned the dominance of the medical framework, let alone begun to provide experiential accounts of disability within other cultures.

In emphasising my own marginalisation within the sociological community, I am not seeking to deny that marginalisation is a significant experience for disabled people within society as a whole. Indeed, a central aim of this book is to begin to explain why this marginalisation of disabled people within society has been made much harder precisely because of the marginalisation of disability within sociology, social anthropology and a variety of other academic disciplines.

Anyone interested in the history of disability will encounter exactly the same problem. On the experience of disability, history is largely silent, and when it is discussed at all, it is within the context of the history of medical advances. Just as women and black people have discovered that they must write their own histories, so too with disabled people. Only then will we have an adequate framework in which to locate our present discussions.

The point of this preamble is to indicate the magnitude of the task involved in attempting to produce a sociology, anthropology or history of disability. In the context of this book, I am certainly not attempting to write the sociology of disability because, for the reasons indicated above, this is an impossible task at present. My aim is much more limited; to begin to apply sociological perspectives to the issue of disability as the basis for ultimately producing nothing less than a social theory of disability.

In beginning to apply these perspectives, I started with the basic question; why is disability individualised and medicalised within capitalist society? This gives rise to a number of other questions, the first of which is whether disability is individualised and medicalised in all societies. If the answer to this is no, then it raises two further questions; how did individualisation and medicalisation come about within capitalism and further, what are the chances of mounting challenges to this individualisation and medicalisation within this type of society? These then are the basic issues to be addressed and they will be done in the following way.

The first chapter will raise as a central concern the issue of meaning. It will look at the meaning of disability by focusing on the debate that has gone on in recent years over how disability should be defined for official purposes and, indeed, the purpose and function of official definitions. Finally, it will consider the arguments of disabled people themselves, who suggest that the meaning of disability is distorted rather than captured by these official definitions.

The second chapter will consider whether the current dominant conception of disability as an individual or medical problem is universal or whether other societies perceive and define disability differently. Drawing upon anthropological material it will be suggested that definitions of disability, as with definitions of other social problems, are related both to economic and social structures and to the central values of particular societies.

The issue of why disability is viewed as an individual problem in capitalist society will be discussed in the third chapter. The functional needs of capital for a particular kind of work force, the relationship between supply and demand for labour and the role of disabled people in the economy will be discussed. It will be suggested that this view of disability is ultimately produced by the functional needs of capital for a particular kind of work force.

The fourth chapter will consider the role of ideology as central to a proper understanding of disability within capitalist society. The influence of particular groups upon these ideological constructions will be discussed, both in historical and current context. The links between ideologies of individualism and medicalisation will be analysed as being contingent upon the rise of the medical profession and the powerful position it currently occupies within capitalism. The implications for the particular kind of discourse this has created about disability will then be examined.

The personal responses of disabled people within this ideological climate will be considered in the next chapter. Adjustment is usually conceived as the process of the individual coming to terms with his disability, rather than one in which society adjusts to the changed requirements of the individual. It will be suggested that there is no universal process but rather that adjustment is an interactive process related, not just to personal biography or stigma, but to structural features as well, notably race and gender.

Chapter 6 will suggest that the responses of disabled people to disability need to be placed within the policy context within which they occur. The influence of social policy responses to disability will be analysed and it will be argued that these responses create rather than reduce dependency. This has facilitated discussions about crises in the welfare state and its subsequent restructuring because of the perceived economic burdens of dependency-creating policies.

Partly as a response to this restructuring, as well as to a growing awareness of the inadequacies of service provision for disabled people, there has arisen what might be called the politics of disablement. Chapter 7 will consider this from the position of traditional political activities; that is, through the participation of disabled people in party politics and traditional pressure group activities. The final chapter will then consider the rise of the disability movement as part of the broader phenomenon of new social movements which characterise capitalism in the late twentieth century.

Before proceeding with the detail of the analysis to be presented, there are a number of disclaimers that need to be made.

The first disclaimer concerns the use of language in this book. Throughout, the term 'disabled people' is used in preference to 'people with disabilities'. It is sometimes argued, often by able-bodied professionals and some disabled people, that 'people with disabilities' is the preferred term, for it asserts the value of the person first and the disability then becomes merely an appendage. This liberal and humanist view flies in the face of reality as it is experienced by disabled people themselves who argue that far from being an appendage, disability is an essential part of the self. In this view it is nonsensical to talk about the person and the disability separately and consequently disabled people are demanding acceptance as they are, as disabled people.

The second disclaimer concerns precisely what is meant by the term 'disabled people'. Is mental handicap included, and blindness and deafness and non-visible disabilities like epilepsy? An adequate social theory of disability as social restriction must reject the categories based upon medical or social scientific constructions and divorced from the direct experience of disabled people. All disabled people experience disability as social restriction, whether those restrictions occur as a consequence of inaccessible built environments, questionable notions of intelligence and social competence, the inability of the general population to use sign language, the lack of reading material in braille or hostile public attitudes to people with non-visible disabilities.

The third disclaimer concerns the use of the term capitalist society in preference to industrial, modern or other such terminology. There are obviously many differences in the ways capitalism has developed, not just between the east and the west, but also within the west itself. This has produced many varieties of social policies and welfare states which have their effects on definitions and experiences of disability. However, it will be argued later that there is an underlying logic to the development of capitalism which creates disability as an individual and medical problem. Unfortunately not enough empirical material exists to undertake an adequate comparative study of disability within various capitalist countries, and this book will have to be judged on the coherence of the argument advanced rather than the evidence it marshals. If a coherent argument and framework does emerge, then it could, of course, provide the framework for a proper comparative study.

One final disclaimer concerns the style of the book and the audience to which it is addressed. My aim has been to write a book which will both encourage academics to take disability seriously as an analytical category, and to develop a theoretically informed understanding of disablement in society amongst disabled people. The dangers of such an approach are obvious: a book which is regarded as over-simplistic by academics or a book which is regarded as over-complex and mystifying by disabled people. All I can say is that in writing this book, I have fulfilled a personal need to bring my own discipline of sociology and my own experience of disability closer together; whether I have succeeded in rendering disability relevant to sociology and sociology intelligible to disabled people is another question.

1
Disability Definitions: the Politics of Meaning

The issue of meaning has been a central one in discussions of differences between the natural and social worlds and the generation of appropriate methodologies to understand these worlds. As far as the social sciences themselves are concerned, the debate around this issue has centred on the violation of meaning through the imposition of inappropriate theoretical perspectives or the ignoring of meaning through the collection of non-reflexive and abstracted data.

Many years ago Wright Mills (1970) criticised the work of social scientists for either being grand theory or abstracted empiricism. The subsequent case for a methodological middle way has had a profound effect on social scientific work ever since and there have been few areas, subjects or topics where theory and empiricism have not met. One exception however, has been the area of disability, to which little attention has been paid. There have been notable exceptions of course, including Topliss (1979), Blaxter (1980), Leonard (1984) and Borsay (1986a) who have approached the area from functionalist, interactionist, Marxist and Weberian positions. However Wright Mills' earlier indictment of social science in general is just as valid today in the area of disability as it was all those years ago.

Thus, while it cannot be claimed that there has been much grand theorising about disability, it can be argued that almost all studies of disability have a grand theory underpinning them. That grand theory can be characterised as 'the personal tragedy theory of disability'. It has fallen to disabled people themselves (Finkelstein, 1980; Oliver, 1983) to provide both critiques of this implicit theory and to construct their own alternatives, which might be called 'social oppression theory'.

Abstracted empiricism has proceeded from the same implicit

1

underpinning, firstly by seeing disability as a problem, and then by devising methodological strategies to measure the extent of these problems that disabled individuals have to face. Again it has fallen to disabled people to provide critiques of this (Sutherland, 1981; Oliver, 1987) and to begin to explore alternative methodological strategies.

A major focus for these debates has centred on the issue of definitions of disability and these, therefore have consequently undergone a number of changes and modifications. Starting from the work of Harris (1971) and her national survey of disabled people, a threefold distinction of impairment, disability and handicap was developed. Following various discussions and refinements, a more sophisticated scheme was advanced by Wood (1981) and this was accepted by the World Health Organisation as the basis for classifying illness, disease and disability. However, these definitions have not received universal acceptance, particularly amongst disabled people and their organisations. Before proceeding further, it is necessary to explain why definitions are important and to spell out the precise nature of the criticisms that have been made.

THE IMPORTANCE OF DEFINITIONS

The social world differs from the natural world in (at least) one fundamental respect; that is, human beings give meanings to objects in the social world and subsequently orientate their behaviour towards these objects in terms of the meanings given to them. W. I. Thomas (1966) succinctly puts it thus: 'if men define situations as real, they are real in their consequences'. As far as disability is concerned, if it is seen as a tragedy, then disabled people will be treated as if they are the victims of some tragic happening or circumstance. This treatment will occur not just in everyday interactions but will also be translated into social policies which will attempt to compensate these victims for the tragedies that have befallen them.

Alternatively, it logically follows that if disability is defined as social oppression, then disabled people will be seen as the collective victims of an uncaring or unknowing society rather than as individual victims of circumstance. Such a view will be translated into social policies geared towards alleviating oppression rather than compensating individuals. It almost goes without saying that at present, the individual and tragic view of disability dominates both social interactions and social policies.

A second reason why definitions are important historically centres on the need to identify and classify the growing numbers of the urban poor in modern industrial societies. In this process of identification and classification, disability has always been an important category, in that it offers a legitimate social status to those who can be defined as unable to work as opposed to those who may be classified as unwilling to do so (Stone, 1985). Throughout the twentieth century this process has become ever more sophisticated, requiring access to expert knowledge, usually residing in the ever-burgeoning medical and paramedical professions. Hence the simple dichotomy of the nineteenth century has given way to a whole new range of definitions based upon clinical criteria or functional limitation.

A third reason why definitions are important stems from what might be called 'the politics of minority groups'. From the 1950s onwards, though earlier in the case of alcoholics, there was a growing realisation that if particular social problems were to be resolved, or at least ameliorated, then nothing more or less than a fundamental redefinition of the problem was necessary. Thus a number of groups including women, black people and homo-sexuals, set about challenging the prevailing definitions of what constituted these problems by attacking the sexist and racist biases in the language used to underpin these dominant definitions. They did this by creating, substituting or taking over terminology to provide more positive imagery (e.g. gay is good, black is beautiful, etc.). Disabled people too have realised that dominant definitions of disability pose problems for individual and group identity and have begun to challenge the use of disablist language. Whether it be offensive (cripple, spastic, mongol, etc.) or merely depersonalising (the handicapped, the blind, the deaf, and so on), such terminology has been attacked, and organisations of disabled people have fostered a growing group consciousness and identity.

There is one final reason why this issue of definitions is impor-tant. From the late fifties onwards there was an upswing in the economy and an increasing concern to provide more services for disabled people out of an ever-growing national cake. But clearly, no government (of whatever persuasion) was going to commit itself to a whole range of services without some idea of what the financial consequences of such a commitment might be. Thus, after some pilot work, the Office of Population Censuses and Surveys (OPCS) was commissioned in the late sixties to carry out a national survey in Britain which was published in 1971 (Harris, 1971). Subsequent work in the international context (Wood, 1981) and more recently a further survey in this country, which has recently been published (Martin, Meltzer and Elliot, 1988), built on and extended this work. However, this work has proceeded isolated from the direct experience of disability as experienced by disabled people themselves, and this has led to a number of wide-ranging and fundamental criticisms of it.

CRITICISMS OF OFFICIAL DEFINITIONS

This work attempts to operationalise a broadly similar conceptual framework and hence criticisms of one can be applied to them all. Specific criticisms of the WHO scheme have focused on the fact that it remains close to medical classifications of disease – disability – handicap. In so doing it conserves the notion of impairment as abnormality in function, disability as not being able to perform an activity considered normal for a human being and handicap as the inability to perform a normal social role. This reification of the idea of normality ignores the issue of what normality actually is, but even if the idea of normality is conceded, the failure to recognise the situational and cultural relativity of normality is a serious ommission in an international scheme (Nordenfelt, quoted in OECD, 1987, p. 5). Similar criticism can be made of the OPCS schemes, in that they fail to recognise the influences of sub-cultures, gender or ethnicity on the idea of normality.

Further, the WHO and OPCS definitions take the environment for granted even though the handicap is no longer considered to be within the individual. As long as the environment consists of social roles that are considered to be normal, the inability of the individual to live up to the requirements of these roles puts him or her in a disadvantaged position and thus creates a handicap. In this way the medical approach is conserved since changes must be brought to bear on the individual rather than the environment (Soder, quoted in OECD, 1987, p. 5).

At this point it is, perhaps, important to clarify what is wrong with the medical approach to disability and to emphasise the word disability. It is not being argued that the medical approach to illness or impairment is inappropriate, although some specific individual medical interventions may well be, but rather that

> The problem ... is that medical people tend to see all difficulties solely from the perspective of proposed treatments for a 'patient', without recognising that the individual has to weigh up whether this treatment fits into the overall economy of their life. In the past especially, doctors have been too willing to suggest medical treatment and hospitalisation, even when this would not necessarily improve the quality of life for the person concerned. Indeed, questions about the quality of life have sometimes been portrayed as something of an intrusion upon the purely medical equation. (Brisenden, 1986, p. 176)

Hence this medical approach produces definitions of disability which are partial and limited and which fail to take into account wider aspects of disability.

A major reason for this has been the failure of the medical profession, and indeed all other professions, to involve disabled people in a meaningful way except as passive objects of intervention, treatment and rehabilitation. This has not just trapped professionals within the medical approach but has had oppressive consequences for disabled people.

> Much of the work which has already been done on definitions has been carried out by people who do not themselves experience the daily problems of disability. This has directly affected the solutions, and in turn has often served to perpetuate discrimination against us, as well as wasting resources on an enormous scale. (Davis, 1986a, p. 2)

A further criticism of both the WHO and OPCS schemes is that, in attempting to make concrete that which is not and can never be, they present disability as a static state and violate its situational and experiential components.

By trying to find strict measures of disability or focussing on 'severe' 'visible' handicaps we draw dividing lines and make distinctions where matters are very blurry and constantly changing. By agreeing that there are twenty million disabled or 36 million, or even that half the population are in some way affected by disability, we delude ourselves into thinking there is some finite, no matter how large, number of people. In this way, both in the defining and in the measuring, we try to make the reality of disease, disability and death problematic, and in this way make it at least potentially someone else's problem. (Zola, 1981, p. 242)

Because of these fundamental flaws, Disabled People's International has opposed the WHO scheme since its inception. Finkelstein, as the then Chair of its national counterpart, the British Council of Organisations of Disabled People, gives the folowing reasoning:

I remained convinced, however, that this classification system in its present form reinforces medical and administrative approaches towards us and that in this respect, it is not in our best interests to support it. (Finkelstein, 1985)

Not only do these definitions medicalise and individualise the problems of disability but they do the same to the solutions (policies) that are applied. Thus services too are based upon an individualised and medicalised view of disability and are designed by able-bodied people through a process over which disabled people have had little or no control. Hence, we come to politics and the oppressive consequences that such definitions and the research based on them, can have for disabled people.

THE POLITICS OF MEANING

It could be argued that in polarising the tragic and oppressive views of disability, a conflict is being created where none necessarily exists. Disability has both individual and social dimensions and that is what official definitions from Harris (1971) through to WHO (Wood, 1981) have sought to recognise and to operationalise. The problem with this, is that these schemes, while acknowledging that there are social dimensions to disability, do not see disability as arising from social causes. Ultimately their rationale rests upon the impaired individual and the social dimensions of disability and handicap arise as a direct consequence of individual impairments.

This view of disability can and does have oppressive consequences for disabled people and can be quite clearly shown in the methodology adopted by the recent OPCS survey in Britain (Martin *et al.*, 1988). The following is a list of questions drawn from the face-to-face interview schedule of this survey.

TABLE 1.1 Survey of disabled adults – OPCS, 1986

Can you tell me what is wrong with you?

What complaint causes your difficulty in holding, gripping or turning things?

Are your difficulties in understanding people mainly due to a hearing problem?

Do you have a scar, blemish or deformity which limits your daily activities?

Have you attended a special school because of a long-term health problem or disability?

Does your health problem/disability mean that you need to live with relatives or someone else who can help look after you?

Did you move here because of your health problem/disability?

How difficult is it for you to get about your immediate neighbourhood on your own?

Does your health problem/disability prevent you from going out as often or as far as you would like?

Does your health problem/disability make it difficult for you to travel by bus?

Does your health problem/disability affect your work in any way at present?

These questions clearly ultimately reduce the problems that disabled people face to their own personal inadequacies or functional limitations. It would have been perfectly possible to reformulate these questions to locate the ultimate causes of disability as within the physical and social environments.

This reformulation is not only about methodology or semantics, it is also about oppression. In order to understand this, it is necessary to understand that, according to OPCS's own figures, 2231 disabled people were given face-to-face interviews (Martin *et al.*, 1988, Table 5.2). In these interviews, the interviewer visits the disabled person at

TABLE 1.2 Alternative questions

Can you tell me what is wrong with society?

What defects in the design of everyday equipment like jars, bottles and tins causes you difficulty in holding, gripping or turning them?

Are your difficulties in understanding people mainly due to their inabilities to communicate with you?

Do other people's reactions to any scar, blemish or deformity you may have, limit your daily activities?

Have you attended a special school because of your education authority's policy of sending people with your health problem or disability to such places?

Are community services so poor that you need to rely on relatives or someone else to provide you with the right level of personal assistance?

What inadequacies in your housing caused you to move here?

What are the environmental constraints which make it difficult for you to get about in your immediate neighbourhood?

Are there any transport or financial problems which prevent you from going out as often or as far as you would like?

Do poorly-designed buses make it difficult for someone with your health problem/disability to use them?

Do you have problems at work because of the physical environment or the attitudes of others?

---

home and asks many structured questions in a structured way. It is in the nature of the interview process that the interviewer presents as expert and the disabled person as an isolated individual inexperienced in research, and thus unable to reformulate the questions in a more appropriate way. It is hardly surprising that, given the nature of the questions and their direction that, by the end of the interview, the disabled person has come to believe that his or her problems are caused by their own health/disability problems rather than by the organisation of society. It is in this sense that the process of the interview is oppressive, reinforcing on to isolated, individual disabled people the idea that the problems they experience in everyday living are a direct result of their own personal inadequacies or functional limitations.

But research can have oppressive consequences not simply because disabled people are the passive recipients of the research process but also because such research has failed to improve the quality of life for them, while doing no harm to the career prospects of the researchers. The classic example of this was the often quoted study *A Life Apart* (Miller and Gwynne, 1972) which has been savagely attacked by one such 'passive' recipient.

> It was clear that Miller and Gwynne were definitely not on our side. They were not really on the side of the staff either. They were, in fact, basically on their own side, that is the side of supposedly 'detached', 'balanced', 'unbiased' social scientists, concerned above all with presenting themselves to the powers that be as indispensable in training 'practitioners' to manage the problem of disabled people in institutions. Thus the fundamental relationship between them and the residents was that of exploiters and exploited. (Hunt, 1981, p. 5)

Finally, the theoretical underpinnings of much research on disability have usually been so divorced from the everyday experience of disabled people that

> they have felt victimised by professionals who write articles about the reactions to disability that are based more upon theory than fact. (Trieschmann, 1980, p. xii)

For these reasons more and more disabled people are refusing to participate in research over which they have no control and which they regard as likely to further their oppression.

A WAY FORWARD

This debate over the nature of disability (whether it is ultimately reducible to the functional limitations of disabled individuals or the structural features and social forces of society), is symptomatic of a more general debate that has occurred throughout the history of the social sciences and has centred on the notion of methodological individualism. This can be defined in the following way:

> Methodological individualism is a doctrine about explanation which asserts that all attempts to explain social (or individual) phenomena are to be rejected (or, according to a current, more

sophisticated version, rejected as 'rock-bottom' explanations) unless they are couched wholly in terms of facts about individuals. (Lukes, 1973, p. 110)

Clearly, neither the WHO nor the OPCS's schemes have been able to shake off the shackles of methodological individualism which has been criticised thus;

> Methodological individualism is thus an exclusivist, prescriptive doctrine about what explanations are to look like ... it excludes explanations which appeal to social forces, structural features of society, institutional factors and so on. (Lukes, 1973, p. 122)

As has already been suggested, the social sciences do not have a very good track-record in critically examining dominant definitions of disability nor the policies and practices to which they give rise. This is somewhat surprising, for there is a tradition within the social sciences which has examined some of the definitions, policies and practices based upon methodological individualism and underpinning a whole range of other social problems. What is urgently needed therefore is a social theory of disability, for

> A social theory of disability should be integrated into, rather than separate from, existing social theories. It has to be remembered, however, that personal tragedy theory itself has performed a particular ideological function of its own. Like deficit theory as an explanation of poor educational attainment, like sickness as an explanation of criminal behaviour, like character weakness as an explanation of poverty and unemployment, and like all other victim blaming theories (Ryan, 1971), personal tragedy theory has served to individualise the problems of disability and hence leave social and economic structures untouched. Social science in general and social policy in particular have moved far in rejecting individualistic theories and constructing a range of alternative social ones – let us hope that personal tragedy theory, the last in the line, will soon disappear also, to be replaced by a much more adequate social (oppression) theory of disability. (Oliver, 1986, p. 16)

The purpose of this book, therefore, is to attempt to develop a social theory of disability. A social theory of disability, however, must be located within the experience of disabled people themselves and their attempts, not only to redefine disability but also to construct a political movement amongst themselves and to develop services commensurate with their own self-defined needs. This process of re-definition has already been begun by disabled people who have dispensed with the intricacies and complexities of the definitions discussed earlier and instead propose the following twofold classification.

Impairment lacking part of or all of a limb, or having a defective limb, organism or mechanism of the body;
Disability the disadvantage or restriction of activity caused by a contemporary social organisation which takes no or little account of people who have physical impairments and thus excludes them from the mainstream of social activities. (UPIAS, 1976, pp. 3–4)

What is at stake here is the issue of causation, and whereas previous definitions were ultimately reducible to the individual and attributable to biological pathology, the above definition locates the causes of disability squarely within society and social organisation.

The rest of the book, therefore, will concentrate disability within the context of society and social organisation. It will be argued that the kind of society that one lives in will have a crucial effect on the way the experience of disability is structured. The focus will then shift to consider the ways in which disability is 'produced' as an individual and medical problem within capitalist society. The individual experience of disability within capitalism is itself constrained by some of the structural features of capitalism including ideology, culture and the influence of race and gender as well as by the activities of key groups and institutions (professionals and professions). These influences will be discussed before, finally, issues of social policy, change and politics will be considered as part of broader developments within late capitalism.

2
The Cultural Production of Impairment and Disability

Building upon the distinction made between impairment and disability, it is possible to argue that both are culturally produced. Further, in seeking to develop a social theory of disability it has recently been argued that 'A theory of disability ... then must offer what is essentially a social theory of impairment.' (Abberley, 1987, p. 9)

While, from an epistemological point of view this may be the case, for present purposes it is a social theory of disability as social restriction that is being considered. However, it is possible to show that both impairment and disability are produced in similar ways.

IMPAIRMENT: A STRUCTURED ACCOUNT

Recently it has been estimated that there are some 500 million severely impaired people in the world today, approximately one in ten of the population (Shirley, 1983). These impairments are not randomly distributed throughout the world but are culturally produced.

> The societies men live in determine their chances of health, sickness and death. To the extent that they have the means to master their economic and social environments, they have the means to determine their life chances. (Susser and Watson, 1971, p. 45)

Hence in some countries impairments are likely to stem from infectious diseases, poverty, ignorance and the failure to ensure that existing medical treatments reach the population at risk (Shirley,

1983). In others, impairments resulting from infectious diseases are declining, only to be replaced by those stemming from the ageing of the population, accidents at work, on the road or in the home, the very success of some medical technologies in ensuring the survival of some severely impaired children and adults and so on (Taylor, 1977). To put the matter simply, impairments such as blindness and deafness are likely to be more common in the Third World, whereas heart conditions, spina bifida, spinal injuries and so on, are likely to be more common in industrial societies.

Again, the distribution of these impairments is not a matter of chance, either across different societies or within a single society, for

> Social and economic forces cause disorder directly; they redistribute the proportion of people at high or low risk of being affected; and they create new pathways for the transmission of disorders of all kinds through travel, migration and the rapid diffusion of information and behaviour by the mass communication media. Finally, social forces effect the conceptualisation, recognition and visibility of disorders. A disorder in one place and at one time is not seen as such in another; these social perceptions and definitions influence both the provision of care, the demands of those being cared for, and the size of any count of health needs. (Susser and Watson, 1971, p. 35)

Social class is an important factor here both in terms of the causes of impairments or what Doyal (1979) calls degenerative diseases, and in terms of outcomes, what Le Grand (1978) refers to as longstanding illnesses.

> Just as we know that poverty is not randomly distributed internationally or nationally (Cole and Miles, 1984; Townsend, 1979), neither is impairment, for in the Third World at least

> Not only does disability usually guarantee the poverty of the victim but, most importantly, poverty is itself a major cause of disability. (Doyal, 1983, p. 7)

There is a similar relation in the industrial countries, as is clearly indicated by Townsend's research (1979) in Britain. Hence, if poverty is not randomly distributed and there is an intrinsic link between poverty and impairment, then neither is impairment randomly distributed.

Even a structured account of impairment cannot, however, be reduced to counting the numbers of impaired people in any one country, locality, class or social group, for

> Beliefs about sickness, the behaviours exhibited by sick persons, and the ways in which sick persons are responded to by family and practitioners are all aspects of social reality. They, like the health care system itself, are cultural constructions, shaped distinctly in different societies and in different social structural settings within those societies. (Kleinman, 1980, p. 38)

The discovery of an isolated tribe in West Africa where many of the population were born with only two toes illustrates this point, for this made no difference to those with only two toes or indeed the rest of the population (Barrett and McCann, 1979). Such differences would be regarded as pathological in our society, and the people so afflicted subjected to medical intervention.

In discussing impairment, it was not intended to provide a comprehensive discussion of the nature of impairment but to show that it occurs in a structured way. However

> such a view does not deny the significance of germs, genes and trauma, but rather points out that their effects are only ever apparent in a real social and historical context, whose nature is determined by a complex interaction of material and non-material factors. (Abberley, 1987, p. 12)

This account of impairment challenges the notion underpinning personal tragedy theory, that impairments are chance events happening to unfortunate individuals. What now needs to be considered is the evidence on the cultural production of disability, before considering the ways in which disability (as social restriction) is structured.

CULTURAL CONSIDERATIONS OF DISABILITY

Anthropologists have placed culture at the centre of their enterprise but in looking at disability cross-culturally, it has to be stressed at the outset that an anthropology of disability has not yet been written. Thus, as one anthropologist has noted

> The non-typical, the deviant, and the disdained were characteristically ignored, treated in footnotes, or considered within a quasi-religious mystique of the impure or tainted, a symbolic categorization, rather than universal phenomena integrated into other aspects of life. (Ablon, 1981, p. 5)

Where anthropologists (Foster and Anderson, 1978; Hellman, 1984) have discussed disability, it has been within a framework derived from health and illness, and dominated by the medical model. This is probably because most anthropologists have internalised the personal tragedy theory of disability and have therefore seen disability as a non-problematic category and not one to be subjected to critical analysis.

There have been exceptions of course; in the field of mental handicap Farber (1968) developed the concept of surplus population to explain the social status of mentally handicapped people historically, cross-culturally and contemporaneously, and Edgerton (1967) used anthropological methods to study the effects of stigma on mentally handicapped people within American society. Further, while Farber was able to acknowledge the view of disability as a social imposition rather than a personal limitation, 'the vicissitudes in the life of the mentally retarded individual result primarily from the status and role assigned him'. (Farber, 1968, p. 15) He concluded that the life-chances of mentally handicapped people are determined 'both by being labelled as deviants and by their incompetence' (p. 19).

Edgerton (1976) in his cross-cultural review of deviance suggests that disabled people are troublesome but that 'non-western societies vary in their response' to this trouble; sometimes treating these troublesome people preferentially, sometimes tolerantly, sometimes harshly and sometimes even killing them off. But, for him, the crucial issue is not that societal responses vary, but why this should be so.

> The most relevant issue here is not what causes mental retardation – or blindness, or any other physical disability – but why

some cultures regard it as seriously troublesome and others do not. About this subject, we remain almost wholly ignorant. (Edgerton 1976, pp. 62–3)

With regard to blindness, Gwaltney's (1970) study in a Mexican village showed that it could only be understood in terms of its own culture and not on the basis of pre-existing assumptions about the nature of blindness, a point that has also been made in a comparative study (Scott, 1969). Thus Gwaltney suggests

The prevailing belief that filarially induced blindness is the consequence of omnipotent, divine intervention tends towards the emergence of an essentially accommodative cultural response. (1970, pp. v–vi)

This cultural response was manifested in the provision of child guides for blind people, social accolades for those who were deferential to blind people, social approbrium to those who were not, and an elaborate system of informal social mechanisms to ensure the participation and integration of blind people into the community. Further, there were no attempts through their own indigenous medical technology or sorcery to provide cures for blindness, indicating what was an 'essentially accommodative adjustment to blindness' (Gwaltney, 1967). Thus blindness was not seen as a tragedy that affected particular individuals but as part of the struggle to live in a harsh environment which could impose a number of disasters on the community, and hence blindness was a problem of the community and not for afflicted individuals.

In the case of deafness the claims of the deaf community for the existence of a separate deaf culture (Ladd, 1988) should make deafness an appropriate area for anthropological study. However, few have ventured into this territory, with the notable exceptions of Farb (1975) and Groce (1985). Groce's study of Martha's Vineyard, an island off the New England coastline, shows how deafness can be seen as social restriction rather than personal tragedy. There were a much higher proportion of deaf people on the island because of intermarriage and the presence of a dominant deafness gene. However, the deaf people were not excluded from society and did not forge their own deaf culture, for everyone knew sign language and the society was 'functionally bilingual'. There thus existed few social restrictions on deaf people and they made a considerable contribution to the life of the community. Farb also found that deaf members of the Amazonian tribe he studied were accorded full social inclusion because of the ability of the whole tribe to use sign language.

These studies are important, not simply because they throw light on another culture, but because they highlight the way in which we disable deaf people in our own society. We do this because of our failure to learn how to communicate with them, not their inability to communicate with us. This might sound unrealistic but has to be seen in the context of our attempts to educate our children in other languages, including dead ones, and the recent plans for a national curriculum when all children will be taught a foreign language. Indeed, our failure to perceive signing as another language with all that implies, but instead to see it as a mechanical method of communication which deaf people use, is itself disabling.

There have been few anthropologists who have taken physical disability seriously as an analytical category, although a distinguished anthropologist, Professor Murphy of Columbia, has attempted to locate his own personal experience of disability within an anthropological framework (Murphy, 1987). His book is not an anthropology of disability but a personal account of a journey into disability, not dissimilar to the personal accounts of nineteenth-century anthropologists and their journeys to distant parts of the world and their encounters with strange and exotic peoples. While he acknowledges that disability imposes social restrictions, he does not suggest that disability is caused by social restrictions, and the weaknesses in his explanation of the marginality of disabled people will be discussed later in the chapter.

The central problems, therefore in trying to provide an adequate theoretical and empirical account of disability cross-culturally, stem from the paucity of existing material and the location of what material there is within personal tragedy theory and the medical model. However, by building on the work of those who have taken disability seriously, and by reinterpreting existing material, it is possible to move towards a more structured cross-cultural account of disability.

DISABILITY: A STRUCTURED ACCOUNT

Disabled people have existed in all societies and at any given historical period. However, the kinds of disabling restrictions that existed and the experiences of disabled people, both individually and collectively, have varied from society to society and from age to age. Two anthropologists, who have taken disability seriously as a category for analysis, have noted the difficulties involved in trying to provide appropriate 'ethnological data' on physical disability both because no logical or medical classifications exist cross-culturally and also because the social disabilities of individuals and groups are peculiar to the social conditions of the particular societies concerned.

> For example, carrot-coloured hair is a physical feature and a handicap in certain social situations, but a person with this characteristic is not included in this class. Nor is the symptom itself the only criterion, for though the person afflicted with infantile paralysis may limp as a result of the disease and be deemed to be handicapped, yet the person with an ill-fitting shoe or a boil on his foot may be excluded. When one introduces the concepts of other cultures than our own, then confusion is multiplied. Even assuming the existence of such a class in other societies, its content varies. The disfiguring scar in Dallas becomes a honorific mark in Dahomey. (Hanks and Hanks, 1980, p. 11)

Their contribution is important, not least because they recognise that disability and illness cannot be categorised as if they were the same thing, but they also acknowledge the cultural and situational relativity of both definitions and experiences of disability.

Further, in reviewing material on disability from a wide range of societies they found that the positions of disabled people 'are as varied as any normal group. The gamut runs from ruler to outcast, from warrior to priest, from infant to aged'. (Hanks and Hanks, 1980, p. 12) From this review it is clear that the individualised, tragic view of disability prevalent in modern industrial society is not universal by any means.

Such variations as do occur are not random, however, but are determined by a range of factors two of which Hanks and Hanks focus upon; the social obligations to and the rights of disabled people in a given society. They also recognise the existence of other determinants.

The type of economy is a factor with its varying productive units, need for manpower, amount of surplus and its mode of distribution. The social structure is important, whether egalitarian or hierarchical, how it defines achievement, how it values age and sex. To these may be added the 'Weltanschauung', the position of the group in relation to its neighbours, the esthetic canons and many more functionally related factors. (Hanks and Hanks, 1980, p. 13)

Few, if any anthropologists have taken this work seriously and built upon it in any way, though a sociologist (Safilios-Rothschild, 1970) did attempt to locate her work in a historical and cross-cultural framework, listing no less than seven factors which may influence prejudice towards disabled people.

Unfortunately none of these writers provide a conceptual framework which explains and integrates these differences, so while they may have dispensed with the issue of randomness, the problem of relativism remains. In addition, within the anthropological literature, three theoretical perspectives are drawn on, usually uncritically and often implicitly, in attempting to explain what happens to disabled people. None of these is adequate in itself but they need to be discussed before a more adequate social theory can be advanced.

IMPLICIT THEORIES OF DISABILITY

The first implicit theoretical underpinning stems from the influential work of Evans-Pritchard (1937) and suggests that in societies dominated by religious or magical ways of thinking, disability is likely to be perceived as punishment by the gods or individual disabled people to be seen as victims of witchcraft. For example, the Wapogoro tribe see epilepsy as a phenomenon that fits within their belief system.

Epilepsy is for them something dramatic, frightening and inexplicable. It must therefore be a spirit who has taken possession of the patient. Some epileptics may be regarded with a certain degree of respect on this account. They even can become a mganga should they not be too much affected intellectually. But mostly the spirit possessing them is supposed to be evil. (Aall-Jilek, 1965, p. 64)

Obviously the way disability is perceived will be dependent upon the specific content of the magical or religious beliefs of a given society. The problem with this explanation is that it sees religious or magical beliefs as autonomous and as the sole determining factor in both defining disability and accounting for the way disabled people are treated in a given society. Even amongst the Wapogoro, Aall-Jilek (1965) found it necessary to treat her epileptic patients within the context of their families rather than as individuals requiring specific modern medical treatments. Similarly, a study of Navajo Indians (Rubin *et al.*, 1965) found a high incidence of limping within the population, due to congenital hip disease. But because the Navajo did not believe the condition was either stigmatising or disabling, they rejected all offers of modern medical treatment.

The second underpinning is based on the work of Turner (1967) and develops the concept of 'liminality'. This has recently been used to explain the social position of disabled people in all societies.

The long-term physically impaired are neither sick nor well, neither dead nor fully alive, neither out of society nor wholly in it. They are human beings but their bodies are warped or malfunctioning, leaving their full humanity in doubt. They are not ill, for illness is transitional to either death or recovery... The sick person lives in a state of social suspension until he or she gets better. The disabled spend a lifetime in a similar suspended state. They are neither fish nor fowl; they exist in partial isolation from society as undefined, ambiguous people. (Murphy, 1987, p. 112)

There are two problems with this explanation; to begin with, as has already been suggested, in not all societies are disabled people, either individually or collectively, placed on the margins. In addition, the explanation of the social position of disabled people is reduced to the idea of a binary distinction of human thought (Lévi-Strauss, 1977) or the search for symbolic order (Douglas, 1966). This reductionism, is grounded in

a particular kind of descriptive anthropology ... which sees societies as, in the final analysis, the embodiment not of social and economic relationships, but of thought systems. (Abberley, 1988, p. 306) and further

> it perpetuates the idea of a metaphysical 'otherness', whilst direct-
> ing attention away from the real physical and social differences
> which disadvantage disabled people. (Abberley, 1988, p. 306)

leading to the absurd view that

> There are, however, no strong economic reasons for systematically
> excluding and abasing the physically handicapped. (Murphy,
> 1987, p. 110)

There are, indeed, strong economic reasons for the exclusion of
disabled people and it is the embodiment of these social and
economic relations under capitalism which has led directly to the
exclusion of disabled people within capitalist societies. This is a
theme which will be returned to later.

The third underpinning is what could be termed the 'surplus
population thesis' and argues that in societies where economic
survival is a constant struggle, any weak or dependent members who
threaten this survival will be dealt with. Thus disabled children may
be killed at birth, disabled adults may be forced out of the
community and disabled old people simply left to die. Thus
Rasmussen (1908) cites an example of an Eskimo man and one of his
wives who were badly burned in an explosion. The wife was simply
left to die but; the husband, if he recovered, might again make an
economic contribution, and so was saved. Nevertheless he resolved
the situation by flinging himself into the sea.

However,

> One should not be misled by the simplicity of economic factors in
> this case. The Australians too had a slim margin of surplus,
> practised infanticide but seemed not to have disposed of the
> physically handicapped in this way. Certainly in Australia age
> was a mark of authority as to make this action difficult. The
> Paiute of the Great Basin of North America, who had an almost
> equally precarious existence, neither practised infanticide nor
> abandoned their disabled. (Hanks and Hanks, 1980, p. 16)

And certainly in relation to mentally handicapped people, both

Farber (1968) and Soder (1984) attempt to go beyond economic determinism and point to the role of values and ideology in shaping social practices, in capitalist societies at least. As has recently been pointed out,

> As the historical record has shown, the definitions of mental retardation have varied in direct correlation with the current social values and economic demands of the defining society. (Manion and Bersani, 1987, p. 236)

TOWARDS A SOCIAL THEORY OF DISABILITY

In attempting to develop a social theory of disability within a sociological framework, it is necessary to stress what is and what is not being attempted. It is not the intention to use the category 'disability' to resolve disputes within sociology itself, whether they be about economic determinism, relative autonomy, ideology or whatever else. Rather the intention is more limited; to show that disability as a category can only be understood within a framework, which suggests that it is culturally produced and socially structured.

Central to this framework is the mode of production, what Hanks and Hanks (1980) refer to as the type of economy and its varying productive units: that is to say, whether a society has an economy based upon hunting and gathering, fishing, agriculture or manufacturing industry, and how it organises the production process, through the household or family unit, the band or the tribe or the individual wage labourer. Obviously the mode of production has important implications for disabled members of a given society. Restricted mobility, for example, is likely to be less life-threatening in an agricultural society than in a nomadic one.

However, as has already been suggested, disability is not defined or culturally produced solely in terms of its relationship to the mode of production. The core or central values may also have a role to play, whether these values are based upon magical, religious or scientific ways of thinking. Thus a society based upon religious or magical ways of thinking may define disability very differently from one based upon science or medicine. Thus, in some societies, someone with polio may be seen as the victim of witchcraft, and someone with epilepsy as possessed by God or the devil. The important implication of this is that disability is not always defined as a personal tragedy with negative consequences; it may be seen as a sign of being chosen, as being possessed by a god, and consequently, the person may have their status enhanced.

Taking both a historical and an anthropological perspective, the position can be summed up as follows;

> Throughout history, discriminatory practices against the sick and disabled have varied greatly from country to country and from century to century; they have ranged from complete rejection and ostracism to semideification and the according of special privileges and honors. (Safilios-Rothschild, 1970, p. 4)

The point has already been made that these differences cannot be explained by chance or cultural relativism, but are culturally produced through the relationship between the mode of production and the central values of the society concerned.

There have been disputes over the precise nature of this relationship, going back at least as far as Marx and Weber. For Marx,

> The mode of production in material life determines the general character of the social, political and spiritual process of life. It is not the consciousness of men that determines their existence but, on the contrary, their social existence that determines their consciousness. (Marx, 1913, p. 266)

Weber (1948) took a less deterministic view and attempted to show how crucial the development of Protestant religious values were in shaping the development of capitalism. This is not the place to enter into these theoretical discussions, but while accepting that primacy must be given to the mode of production, there are other factors which also need to be taken into account.

In considering experiences of disability in different societies, it has been suggested that all disabled people have one thing in common,

> On a material plane the disabled individual is ... less able to adapt to the demands of his environment: he has reduced power to insulate himself from the assaults of an essentially hostile milieu. However, the disadvantage he experiences is likely to differ in relation to the nature of the society in which he finds himself. (Wood and Badley, 1978, p. 149)

Two crucial factors in this are the size of the economic surplus produced by any given society and how this is redistributed amongst the population as a whole.

The size of the economic surplus available for redistribution is important for weak or dependent members: those societies with little or no surplus may be forced to leave individuals to cope for themselves, starve or may even deliberately put people to death. On the other hand, societies which produce very large economic surpluses will almost certainly have established elaborate mechanisms of redistribution; but who gets what amount will be significantly influenced by the iedology underpinning this redistribution process. Modern industrial socieites invariably produce large economic surpluses which are redistributed and a major mechanism for this redistribution is the welfare state. Again, the way in which the welfare state operates is significantly influenced by the ideologies underpinning it (George and Wilding, 1976) and in the case of Britain, the ideology underpinning redistribution for disabled people is personal tragedy theory.

Precisely why this should be so, given that personal tragedy theory is not the only way disability is culturally produced, will be considered later. This chapter has shown that this cultural production of disability is dependent upon a variety of factors including the type of economy, the size of the economic surplus and the values that influence the redistribution of this surplus. The general point to be emphasised is that

> our consciousness of the world is a human construction rather than a merely mechanical reflection of external reality. Furthermore, this human construction of the world as perceived is different in different historical periods and different social groups. (Manning, 1985, p. 23)

Before looking at differences between groups within a particular society we need to look at how services for disabled people have developed from a historical perspective, for 'The history of disability is critical to understanding the contemporary situation and this has been completely ignored.' (Scott, 1976, p. 47)

3

Disability and the Rise of Capitalism

The stressing of the need to provide a theoretical explanation of disability and the importance of developing a historical understanding of it, do not imply the endorsement of the theory of historical materialism, nor its applicability to a proper understanding of the nature of disability, for

> It is not necessary to be a Marxist to recognise that economic conditions have a significant impact on social behaviour and on relationships between different groups of individuals in society. (Harbert, 1988, p. 12)

The previous chapters have suggested that the definitions and experiences of disability vary from society to society depending on a whole range of material and social factors. The crucial issue to be discussed in the next two chapters is why the view of disability as an individual, medical problem and a personal tragedy has been the dominant one in modern capitalist societies.

Given that no adequate social theory of disability has yet been advanced, it is necessary to draw upon the work of some earlier social theorists whose main concern was to develop an understanding of the rise and progress of capitalism. Notwithstanding recent critiques of evolutionary approaches to human history (Giddens, 1984), it will be suggested that such approaches, derived particularly from the work of Marx, Comte and Weber, can at least provide a framework to facilitate our understanding of the present situation in respect of disability.

THE MODE OF PRODUCTION AND HISTORICAL CHANGE

A framework derived from historical materialism does, at least, add to our understanding of what happened to disabled people with the coming of industrial society. A general statement of this view of history is as follows:

> In Marx's view, to understand the nature of human beings one must understand their relationship to the material environment and the historical nature of this relationship in creating and satisfying human needs. This material environment may, in the first instance, be the constraints of the physical environment. However, as societies develop and become more complicated, the environment itself will become more complicated and comprise more socio-cultural constraints. (Forder *et al.*, 1984, p. 89)

These socio-cultural constraints may include the nature of the work environment, the living conditions of people in rural or urban environments and the relationships between institutions, groups and individuals, all of which are related to the socio-economic structure of society at particular points in history.

> So an understanding of historical process makes possible an understanding of human nature and the social relationships which exist at any particular point in time. (Forder *et al.*, 1984, p. 90)

But historical materialism is not just about placing social relationships within a historical setting. It also attempts to provide an evolutionary perspective on the whole of human history, and of particular relevance here are the transitions from feudal through capitalist to socialist society. No attempt has been made to apply this (or indeed any other social theory) to the history of disability, though Finkelstein (1980) has located his account within a materialist framework and developed an evolutionary model, broadly along the lines of the three stages of the historical materialist model mentioned above, though without using the same terminology.

His model is couched in terms of three phases of historical development. Phase 1 corresponds to Britain before the industrial revolution; that is feudal society. Phase 2 corresponds to the process of industrialisation when the focus of work shifted from the home to the factory; that is capitalist society. This takes us up to the present day, and Phase 3 refers to the kind of society to which we are currently moving, though Finkelstein does not spell out the differences between Phases 2 and 3, nor does he comment on whether Phase 3 marks the beginning of the transition to socialism as predicted by historical materialism.

The economic base in Phase 1, agriculture or small-scale industry, did not preclude the great majority of disabled people from participating in the production process, and even where they could not participate fully, they were still able to make a contribution. In this era disabled people were regarded as individually unfortunate and not segregated from the rest of society. With the rise of the factory in Phase 2, many more disabled people were excluded from the production process for

> The speed of factory work, the enforced discipline, the time-keeping and production norms – all these were a highly unfavourable change from the slower, more self-determined and flexible methods of work into which many handicapped people had been integrated. (Ryan and Thomas, 1980, p. 101)

As capitalism developed, this process of exclusion from the workforce continued for all kinds of disabled people.

> By the 1890's, the population of Britain was increasingly urban and the employment of the majority was industrial, rather than rural. The blind and the deaf growing up in slowly changing scattered rural communities had more easily been absorbed into the work and life of those societies without the need for special provision. Deafness, while working alone at agricultural tasks that all children learned by observation with little formal schooling, did not limit the capacity for employment too severely. Blindness was less of a hazard in uncongested familiar rural surroundings, and routine tasks involving repetitive tactile skills could be learned and practised by many of the blind without special training. The environment of an industrial society was however different. (Topliss, 1979, p. 11)

Changes in the organisation of work from a rural based, cooperative system where individuals contributed what they could to the production process, to an urban, factory-based one organised around the individual waged labourer, had profound consequences. 'The operation of the labour market in the nineteenth century effectively depressed handicapped people of all kinds to the bottom of the market. (Morris, 1969, p. 9)

As a result of this, disabled people came to be regarded as a social and educational problem and more and more were segregated in institutions of all kinds including workhouses, asylums, colonies and special schools, and out of the mainstream of social life. The emergence of Phase 3, according to Finkelstein, will see the liberation of disabled people from the segregative practices of society largely as a consequence of the utilisation of new technologies and the working together of professionals and disabled people towards common goals. Whether this is likely to be so, is an issue which will be returned to in later chapters.

For Finkelstein, disability is a paradox involving the state of the individual (his or her impairment) and the state of society (the social restrictions imposed on an individual). By adopting a three-stage evolutionary perspective, he sees the paradox emerging in Phase 2. In Phase 1 disabled individuals formed part of a larger underclass but in Phase 2 they were separated from their class origins and became a special, segregated group, whereby the paradox emerged and disability came to be regarded both as individual impairment and social restriction. Phase 3, which is just beginning, sees the end of the paradox whereby disability comes to be perceived solely as social restriction.

Like historical materialism, this model has explanatory power particularly in helping us to understand what happened in Phase 2 or with the emergence of capitalist society. However, it does tend to oversimplify what was happening prior to this capitalist emergence. It implies that in Phase 1, some kind of idealised community existed and that disabled people, amongst other minority groups, were treated more benignly. While it is certainly true that the emergence of capitalism had profound effects on social relations generally and that many acceptable social roles and positions disappeared, and that this directly affected disabled people in many instances, it is difficult to assess whether these changes affected the quality of the experience of disability negatively or positively, largely because history is silent on the experience of disability.

A similar model has been advanced to explain variations in social responses to and personal experiences of disability in the modern world (Sokolowska *et al.*, 1981). They suggest that there are three kinds of society in the modern world; what they call developing, intermediary-developed and highly-developed or types I, II and III. Type I societies are characterised by the spontaneous participation of disabled people; type II societies are characterised by the separation of disabled people from the rest of society; and type III societies are, or should be, characterised by the integration of disabled people, made possible by the supply of 'necessary appliances'.

This contemporary model, like Finkelstein's historical one, is of considerable value in highlighting the importance of the mode of production in significantly influencing perceptions and experiences of disability. However, both models are over-simplistic and over-optimistic. They are over-simplistic in that they assume a simple relationship between the mode of production and perceptions and experiences of disability, without considering a range of other influential factors, many of which were discussed in the previous chapter. They are also too optimistic in that both assume that technological developments will liberate disabled people and integrate them back into society. The ambiguities of the role of technology in modern society will be returned to in Chapter 8, but for now, we need to consider some of the other factors which influence perceptions and experiences of disability.

THE MODE OF THOUGHT AND HISTORICAL CHANGE

Auguste Comte also provided an evolutionary model aimed at providing an understanding of the development of human history. He suggested that the human intellectual process could be understood in terms of three stages of development; the theological, the metaphysical and the positivistic stages. This model suggests that there has been a shift from a religious interpretation of reality to a more naturalistic one and finally to a scientific way of understanding both the natural and social worlds:

each branch of our understanding passes through three different stages: the theological or fictitious stage; the metaphysical or abstract stage; and the scientific or positive stage. In other words, the human mind, by its very nature, employs successively in each of its fields of investigation three methods of philosophising whose character is essentially different and even radically opposed: first, the theological method, next the metaphysical method, and finally the positive method. This gives rise to three kinds of philosophy or of general conceptual systems about all phenomena which are mutually exclusive. (Comte, 1855, p. 2)

This evolutionary model has proved useful in developing an understanding of changing historical perceptions of deviance (Kittrie, 1971) including drug addiction, homosexuality, alcoholism and mental illness; each being regarded first as moral, then legal and now medical problems. As a result of these perceptions particular deviants were subjected to moral, then legal and now medical mechanisms of social control. Similarly, a recent review of the medicalisation of deviance suggests

that three major paradigms may be identified that have held reign over deviance designations in various historical periods: deviance as sin; deviance as crime and deviance as sickness. (Conrad and Schneider, 1980, p. 27)

There have been few attempts to utilise this evolutionary model to develop an understanding of changing historical perceptions of disability. However, a recent analysis of the ideology of care underlying the development of services for mentally handicapped people suggests a similar approach (Soder, 1984). This analysis suggests that initially the care provided was based upon a philosophy of compassion linked to religious and philanthropic perspectives; then services were provided based upon the philosophy of protection, both for the disabled individuals and society; and finally care was provided on the basis of optimism, linked to the development of new scientific and pedagogic approaches to the problem of mental handicap.

Comte's model has also been used to illustrate changing patterns of prejudice in respect of people with epilepsy:

increasing rationalisation did not ameliorate social prejudice against epileptics – it merely caused one form of prejudice to be substituted for another. He was no longer isolated as unclean, as a ritually untouchable person, but instead he was isolated as insane, and placed in institutions where he was subjected to extremely substandard conditions of life. However later evidence suggests that further rationalisation and increasing knowledge of the causation of epilepsy, separating it from insanity, may lead to improvements in social conditions for epileptics – as the culture catches up with findings of the scientific community. (Pasternak, 1981, p. 227)

This optimism mirrors optimism found in the work of Comte and in Soder's analysis of mental handicap, but whether this is justified in respect of the medicalisation of disability will be returned to in the next chapter. For now we need to consider two criticisms of this evolutionary model and its application, one internal and the other external.

The internal criticism of these models is that the 'phenomena' are not 'mutually exclusive' as Comte implies. While one perception may dominate at a particular point in history, it does not do so at the expense of the others. In modern industrial societies, people with epilepsy may still be perceived by some as possessed by demons, still subject to legal regulation (with regard to marriage, work or driving) and yet be the recipients of sophisticated medical treatments of one kind or another (Oliver, 1979). Similarly, the explanation for the birth of a disabled child will clearly be a medical or scientific one, but that does not mean that some parents may not feel that it is a punishment for some previous sin. Thus, while the model may add to our understanding of changing perceptions of deviance and disability, it cannot and does not explain them, in causal terms, at least.

The external criticism concerns this issue of causality and takes us back to the Marx/Weber debate and it is clear that changing perceptions of epilepsy cannot be accounted for solely in terms of the mode of thought for

The drift to the town and the growing complexity of industrial machinery at the time meant the development of a class of industrial rejects for whom it was clear that special provision would have to be made... The problem of severe epileptics in a city such as Bradford, where the wool trade meant fast moving machinery, and crowded workshops, must have been particularly acute. (Jones and Tillotson, 1965, pp. 5–6)

Hence the nature of disability can only be understood by using a model which takes account of both changes in the mode of production and the mode of thought, and the relationship between them. What now needs to be considered is this relationship between the two, and the ways in which the economic surplus is redistributed through social policies which both meet the needs of the changing mode of production and which are commensurate with current social perceptions about what are, and are not, appropriate ways of dealing with this problem.

STATE INTERVENTION IN THE LIVES OF DISABLED PEOPLE

The rise of capitalism brought profound changes in the organisation of work, in social relations and attitudes, and these changes had implications for family life. These factors, with the demographic explosion which accompanied them, posed new problems for social order and with the breakdown of traditional social relations, new problems of classification and control.

The main solution to this problem was the institution (Rothman, 1971), and while institutions existed in feudal times, it was with the rise of capitalism that the institution became the major mechanism of social control. Thus there was a proliferation of prisons, asylums, workhouses, hospitals, industrial schools and colonies. The institution was a remarkably successful vehicle in dealing with the problem of imposing order and it was in accord with changing social values consequent upon the 'civilising process' (Elias, 1977) and the switch from 'punishment of the body to punishment of the mind' (Foucault, 1977). The institution was successful because it embodied both repressive and ideological mechanisms of control (Althusser, 1971). It was repressive in that it offered the possibility of forced removal from the community for anyone who refused to conform to the new order. But it was ideological also, in that it acted as a visible monument, replacing the public spectacle of the stocks, the pillory and the gallows, to the fate of those who would not or could not conform.

Total institutions work their effects on society through the mythic and symbolic weight of their walls on the world outside, through the ways, in other words, in which people fantasize, dream and fear the archipelago of confinement. (Ignatieff, 1983, p. 169)

It was not just the prisons and asylums which operated as mechanisms of social control; the workhouse as well was crucial, and its ideological function was always more important than its repressive one:

> the workhouse represented the ultimate sanction. The fact that comparatively few people came to be admitted did not detract from the power of its negative image, an image that was sustained by the accounts that circulated about the harsh treatment and separation of families that admission entailed. The success of 'less eligibility' in deterring the able bodied and others from seeking relief relied heavily on the currency of such images. Newspapers, songs and gossip, as well as orchestrated campaigns for the abolition or reform of the system, all lent support to the deliberate attempts that were made to ensure that entry to a workhouse was widely regarded as an awful fate. (Parker, 1988, p. 9)

In the institution, the state had found a successful method of dealing with the problem of order, and in the workhouse, a successful method of imposing discipline on the potential workforce. But it still faced the age-old problem of separating out those who would not from those who could not conform to the new order. Hence throughout the eighteenth and nineteenth centuries institutions became ever more specific in their purposes and selective in their personnel. This distinction between the deserving and the undeserving, which has shaped the development of welfare policies throughout history, has never been satisfactorily resolved.

These developments then, facilitated the segregation of disabled people, initially in workhouses and asylums, but gradually in more specialist establishments of one kind or another:

> the rise of specialist asylums signified an important shift in the way in which the poor, dependent and deviant were contained . . . Public workhouses, as opposed to domestic relief, were increasingly used for all those who could not or would not support themselves

economically. In these, idiots, lunatics, the chronic sick, the old and vagrants were mixed up with allegedly able-bodied unemployment. (Ryan and Thomas, 1980, p. 100)

However, it quickly became clear that workhouses could not simply function as residual dumping grounds for such disparate groups of people. A crucial issue was that of separating out those who could not work from those who could but would not; effective discipline and deterrence required these groups to be separated from each other. But further separation and specialisation was necessary within the former group in order to successfully manage and control this group in ways that were socially acceptable at the time.

The Poor Law Amendment Act (1834) played an important part in this process of increasing specialisation and the disability category was crucial in separating out those unwilling from those unable to work.

In the regulations of the Poor Law administration and thus in the eyes of the Poor Law administrators, five categories were important in defining the internal universe of paupers; children, the sick, the insane, 'defectives', and the 'aged and infirm'. Of these, all but the first are part of today's concept of disability. The five groups were the means of defining who was able-bodied; if a person didn't fall into one of them, he was able-bodied by default. This strategy of definition by default remains at the core of current disability programs. None provides positive definition of 'able-bodied'; instead, 'able to work' is a residual category whose meaning can be known only after the 'unable to work' categories have been precisely defined. (Stone, 1985, p. 40)

It would be a mistake to imagine that the success of the institution meant that all or even a majority of disabled people ended up in one. In feudal times the family and the community were the places in which disabled people existed. With the coming of capitalism the family remained the setting where the majority of disabled people lived out their lives. What did change however, partly as a consequence of the ideological climate created by institutions setting people apart from the rest of society, was that disability became a thing of shame; the process of stigmatisation caught the deserving as well as the undeserving. But not all families could cope with

difficulties of having disabled people segregated within them, particularly working-class families which were already under pressure in
the new capitalist social order. Hence disabled people became
segregated from their communities and wider societies and, only
when the families were unwilling or unable to cope, did they become
possible candidates for the institution.

Nobody wanted to go into an institution but not every relative
found it possible to keep their dependent kin, especially so it
seems, the mentally disordered and the aged. (Parker, 1988,
p. 23)

Both the family and the institution, therefore, became places of
segregation. But, as far as the balance between institutional and
family provision for disabled people is concerned

We know next to nothing about this, but it is reasonable to
suppose, for example, that the undoubted decline in domestic
production in the outwork industries, the artisanal sector and the
cottage economy of the agricultural labourer made it more
difficult for poor families, particularly women, to provide domestic care for the aged and insane. (Ignatieff, 1983, p. 172)

Thus, as a consequence of the increasing separation between work
and home, the boundaries of family obligations towards disabled
people were re-drawn; so the new asylums and workhouses met a
need among poor families struggling to cope with 'burdens which for
the first time may have been felt to be unbearable' (Ignatieff, 1983).
This distinction between segregation in the family and in the
institution remained into the twentieth century as the state became
more interventionist and the foundations of the welfare state as we
know it today, developed. As one commentator puts it

The provision of personal care and practical assistance to disabled
people falls into two main divisions, that of residential care and
that of support and assistance to disabled people in their own
homes. (Topliss, 1982, p. 77)

What has changed in the twentieth century has been the balance between institutional and family care. To be sure, there has been a 'de-institutionalisation' or 'decarceration' movement in the latter part of the twentieth century and undoubtedly many people previously in institutions have been returned to the community. The closure, initially of the workhouses and colonies and later the longstay hospitals has undoubtedly put many thousands of those previously incarcerated back into the community; but two points need to be made about this.

Firstly, within the different groups of people who are poor, old sick, disabled, insane and so on, just as the proportions within each group who were institutionalised, were different, so too have been the rates of discharge back into the community. Secondly, while the numbers of people may vary significantly, the ideological shift from institutional to community care has been much more significant. As far as disabled people are concerned, the majority have always lived in the community, albeit sometimes segregated from it, and so perhaps the shift has been more apparent than real. A similar point has recently been made in an analysis of the historical development of social control with the rise of capitalism.

> There have been two transformations – one transparent, the other opaque, one real, the other eventually illusory – in the master patterns and strategies for controlling deviance in Western industrial societies. The first, which took place between the end of the eighteenth and nineteenth centuries, laid the foundations of all deviancy control systems. The second, which is supposed to be happening now, is thought by some to represent a questioning, even a radical reversal of that earlier transformation, by others merely to signify a continuation and intensification of its patterns. (Cohen, 1985, p. 13)

Rather than consider here whether these transformations actually mean a loosening of the structures of social control or not, what now needs to be considered is why these changes took place.

EXPLANATIONS – BACK TO COMTE AND MARX

In seeking to explain, rather than merely describe, what happened to disabled people with the coming of capitalist society, it should be pointed out that both the movement to institutional care and the movement away from it will be incorporated within the same explanatory framework.

The first explanation draws heavily on the Comtean framework and suggests that what happened to disabled people, and others, can be seen as the progressive evolution of reason and humanity, and that the move from community to institution and back again, reflects changing ideas about social progress. This view is what Abrams (1982) calls 'the enlightenment theory of social welfare' and incorporates the establishment of segregated institutions in Benthamite terms as improvements on earlier forms of provision. Further it also incorporates variants of the anti-institution movement of the late twentieth century, sparked off by the work of Goffman (1961) and a number of damning public enquiries about the conditions in longstay hospitals, suggesting that the move back to community care reflects our changing ideas abut the appropriateness of institutional provision in modern society.

What it fails to explain, however, is that many of those confined to institutions experienced this as punishment rather than treatment, and indeed, as recent studies have made clear (Scull, 1977), return to the community can also be an extremely punitive experience. Changing ideas about the nature of the institution and of community incorporated in the enlightenment theory are thus

> too one-dimensional to be altogether satisfactory. It recognises, one might say, that men make their own history but not the equally important fact that they do not make it just as they please. Of course men act on the basis of ideas but the ideas they have at any particular time and still more the influence of these ideas is not just an intellectual matter. Many good ideas never get a hearing; many bad ideas flourish for generations. (Abrams, 1982, pp. 11–12)

The success or failure of these ideas are dependent upon a whole range of other factors such as the economic and social conditions under which they develop and the support or resistance they encounter from people in powerful political positions and institutions.

The second explanation draws on the Marxian model and suggests that changes in policy and provision for disabled people were determined by changes in the mode of production. Thus

> The asylums of the nineteenth century were ... as much the result of far-reaching changes in work and family life, and corresponding methods of containing the poor, as they were the inspiration of philanthropists and scientists. With other similar institutions of the period, they have remained the main alternative to the family ever since. (Ryan and Thomas, 1980, p. 101)

Similarly, the change back to community care was not simply the product of anti-institution ideas, which had been around in the nineteenth as well as the twentieth centuries, but also because 'segregative modes of social control became ... far more costly and difficult to justify' (Scull, 1977, p. 135).

This explanation is what Abrams (1982) calls 'the necessity theory of social welfare' and incorporates not just the economic rationality underpinning much social provision but also the need to impose and maintain order in the changing industrial world. While this theory

> forces us to pay attention to the ways in which social facts and conditions constrain and impel men to act in certain ways ... it corrects the bland tendency of enlightenment theory to detach ideas from their social context. But at the same time it tends to deny the equally important fact that what men do in the face of even the most constraining social conditions is indeed something they choose to do. (Abrams, 1982, pp. 12–13)

But neither the institution nor community care can be explained solely in terms of humanitarianism or necessity. The 'action theory of welfare' is also important and Parker (1988), in his historical review of residential care, suggests two factors of relevance. Firstly he suggests that the willingness, or otherwise, of families to care for their dependents was important and he cites historians like Ignatieff (1983) who have claimed that 'the working class family have played an active rather than a passive part, in the history of institutional development'. Thus he suggests that

> the level of demand for institutional care seems to have been a function of (a) the acceptability of that care as perceived by relatives; (b) the costs which they consider they and their families bear in continuing to look after the dependent or disruptive

member; and (c) the number of dependent people without close relatives. (Parker, 1988, p. 24)

Some families have also played an active part in seeking to have relatives removed from longstay hospitals, special schools and children's homes, though as the defects in community care become more and more apparent, other families are actively campaigning for institutions to remain.

Secondly, he suggests that institutions have been important historically because of the role they have played in campaigns of rescue, notably of children in the latter half of the nineteenth century. This rescue mission was also an important factor in the development of residential care for disabled people after the Second World War, when the Cheshire Foundation supposedly 'rescued' many disabled adults from isolation in families, from longstay hospitals, from geriatric wards and other unsuitable provision. That history may subsequently reinterpret such action as incarceration rather than rescue does not invalidate the actions of individuals at particular historical points.

Thus while the 'action theory of welfare' may not explain the forms that provision may take when extracted from historical context, it is useful in developing an understanding of the precise nature and form of that provision, consequent upon the influence of individuals, families and groups at a particular point in time. However, what the action theory does not explain, according to Abrams (1982), is that some groups 'prove persistently more influential than others', necessitating the development of a 'power theory of welfare'. Undoubtedly the group that has been most persistently influential in the context of disability, has been the medical profession and this will be discussed more fully in the following chapter. Before that, there is one further explanation which needs to be discussed and this draws upon Weberian notions of rationality, though it does also incorporate elements of the necessity theory.

RATIONALISATION – DISABILITY AS AN ADMINISTRATIVE CATEGORY

The work of Stone (1985) is different from that discussed previously in this chapter in that it takes disability itself seriously as a theoretical category and grounds its theorising in a discussion of the development of welfare policies in respect of disability in Britain, the USA and Germany. While making no reference to the work of Weber, the argument she presents can be located in his notion of the development of capitalism being accompanied by an increasing 'rationalisation' of the world. Weber's approach can be summarised thus:

> By 'rationalisation' Weber meant the process by which explicit, abstract, calculable rules and procedures are increasingly substituted for sentiment, tradition and rule of thumb in all spheres of activity. Rationalisation leads to the displacement of religion by specialised science as a major source of intellectual authority; the substitution of the trained expert for the cultivated man of letters; the ousting of the skilled handworker by machine technology; the replacement of traditional judicial wisdom by abstract, systematic statutory codes. Rationalisation demystifies and instrumentalises life. (Wrong, 1970, p. 26)

In respect of provision to meet the changing needs of disabled people with the development of capitalism, this was done through the elaboration of ever more detailed systems of bureaucratic organisation and administration.

Stone's (1985) basic argument is that all societies function through the 'distributive principle' in that goods and services produced have to be allocated amongst the population as a whole. The major mechanism of distribution (and production) is work, but not everyone is able or willing to work. Thus a distributive system based on need will also exist and the 'distributive dilemma' centres on how to allocate goods and services based upon the very different principles of work and need. With the rise of capitalism, disability has become an important boundary category through which people are allocated either to the work-based or needs-based system of distribution. The increasing specialisation of both categorisation and provision is thus a function of the increasing rationalisation of the world.

This explanation incorporates elements of necessity theory, both in the need to redistribute goods and services and in relation to labour supply.

The disability concept was essential to the development of a workforce in early capitalism and remains indispensable as an instrument of the state in controlling labor supply. (Stone, 1985, p. 179)

However, it fails to acknowledge the contradictory aspects of rationalisation noted by Weber in the distinction he makes between formal rationality and substantive rationality (Weber, 1968) and the way the latter may contradict the former. It is possible to argue, as Stone does, that the formal rationality underpinning the disability category makes it the ascription of privilege, in that it offers legitimate social status to those classified as unable to work. But the substantive rationality, enshrined in the experience of disability, is much more concerned with the processes of stigmatisation and oppression.

Stone acknowledges the contradictions inherent in the development of capitalism discussed both by Marx and Weber, and discusses what she calls 'economic and political versions of contradiction theory'. In the economic version, the state experiences a fiscal crisis because it must constantly expand its expenditures while its revenues cannot grow fast enough to meet these expenditures. The political version stresses 'legal rights to social aid' which engenders political support from some sections of society but opposition from others. Both versions predict eventual system breakdown because of either economic crises or the erosion of political support. However, by concentrating on the boundaries between various parts of the capitalist system, rather than on its internal logic she concludes that

> The interpretation of disability as a concept that mediates the boundary between two conflicting distributive principles offers a very different answer to the question of co-existence. (Stone, 1985, p. 20)

The answer, at least in the short term, therefore, is that the disability category, because it is socially constructed and flexible, can resolve any systemic contradictions that may occur.

By the late twentieth century, however, Stone notes that the disability category has become less flexible as the standards for eligibility get more and more detailed; once certain groups are accepted into the category they cannot be ejected from it; people

become socialised into their role as disabled; and disability categorisation is legitimated by the medical and welfare bureaucracies. This
has provoked a crisis in disability programmes which may not be
subject to categorical resolution, for

> Keepers of the category will have to elaborate ever more situa-
> tions in which people are legitimately needy, until the categories
> became so large as to engulf the whole. (Stone, 1985, p. 192)

If such a situation were to occur, where the distributive dilemma
was resolved on the basis of need, then that would surely mark the
transition from capitalism to socialism predicted by Marx. But that
is to go too far, too fast, and we need to resume the consideration of
what disability under capitalism is actually like rather than consider
what it might be like under socialism.

This chapter has attempted to discuss disability in the context of
the rise of capitalist society and has suggested that economic
development, the changing nature of ideas and the need to maintain
order, have all influenced social responses to and the experience of
it. The rise of the institution as a mechanism of both social provision
and social control has played a key role in structuring both
perceptions and experiences of disability, and facilitated the exclusion of disabled people from the mainstream of social life. Within
this, the ideological dimension has been at least as important as the
physical provision of segregated establishments and it is precisely
this ideological dimension which is now being challenged with the
development of community care. What needs to be considered next
is the way the individualisation of life under capitalism has contributed to the individualisation of disability and the role of powerful
groups, notably, the medical profession, in this process.

4

The Ideological Construction of Disability

No attempt to develop a social theory of disability can ignore the issue of ideology for

> there is a clear relationship between prevailing social structures, dominant ideology and the way society handles its deviants. (Abbot and Sapsford, 1987, p. 7)

But part of the problematic for social theory is that there is no one universally agreed definition of ideology, and indeed, in some definitions, the very nature of ideology is to obscure the relationship between social structures, social policies and the treatment of deviants.

Here, ideology will be characterised by a set of values or beliefs underpinning social practices, whether those social practices be the work process, medical intervention or the provision of welfare services. But that itself is not enough, for, by leaving it there, social consciousness can be reduced to a pluralist vision of sets of competing ideologies. Hence it is necessary to turn to the work of Gramsci (1971) who attempted to provide a specific link between social structures and ideologies by distinguishing between what he called 'organic' and 'arbitrary' ideologies.

But, further, he attempted to address the issue of power and dominant ideology through the development of the concept of hegemony which becomes more all-bracing than ideology for

> It is the sheer taken-for-grantedness of hegemony that yields its full affects – the 'naturalness' of a way of thinking about social, economic, political and ethical issues. (Hamilton, 1987, p. 8)

43

The hegemony that defines disability in capitalist society is constituted by the organic ideology of individualism, the arbitrary ideologies
of medicalisation underpinning medical intervention and personal
tragedy theory underpinning much social policy. Incorporated also
are ideologies related to concepts of normality, able-bodiedness and
able-mindedness. These ideologies will be the subject of the next two
chapters and the issue of hegemony will be returned to subsequently.

INDIVIDUALISM AND IDEOLOGY

The ways in which the rise of capitalism excluded disabled people
from the process of work and its consequent social relations was
described in the previous chapter. But it also changed the way
disabled people were viewed, for 'Capitalism, whether free market
or welfare, encourages us to view people . . . as a commodity for sale
in the labour market. (Burton, 1983, p. 67)

The requirements of the capitalist economy were for individuals
to sell their labour in a free market and this necessitated a break
from collectivist notions of work as the product of family and group
involvement. It demanded nothing less than the ideological construction of the individual. Or to put it in a slightly different way,
'Thus individualism is seen as being the ideological foundation upon
which the transition to capitalism was based. (Dalley, 1988, p. 32)
That this ideological construction of the individual was rooted in
history, Marx had no doubt.

> The further back we go into history, the more the individual, and,
> therefore, the producing individual seems to depend on and
> constitute a part of a larger whole: at first it is, quite naturally, the
> family and the clan, which is but an enlarged family; later on, it is
> the community growing up in its different forms out of the clash
> and the amalgamation of clans. (Marx, 1913, p. 267)

Hence, individuals always existed but only as part of larger social
groupings whether they be families, clans or communities. It was
only with the rise of capitalism that the isolated, private individual
appeared on the historical stage.

It is but in the eighteenth century, in 'bourgeois society', that the different forms of social union confront the individual as a mere means to his private ends, as an outward necessity. But the period in which this view of the isolated individual becomes prevalent, is the very one in which the inter-relations of society (general from this point of view) have reached the highest state of development. (Marx, 1913, p. 268)

This highest state of development (that is, the rise of capitalism) did not simply bring with it new problems for social order and social control. It also required new ways of seeing or constructing these problems of order and control.

Within this set of problems, the 'body' – the body of individuals and the body of populations – appears as the bearer of new variables, not merely between the scarce and the numerous, the submissive and the restive, rich and poor, healthy and sick, strong and weak, but also between the more or less utilizable, more or less amenable to profitable investment, those with greater or lesser prospects of survival, death and illness, and with more or less capacity for being usefully trained. (Foucault, 1980, p. 172)

This, then, is the ideological underpinning for the separation and specialisation processes which took place with the rise and development of the institution and which were described in the previous chapter.

Further, as Lukes as pointed out, this ideological construction of, or way of seeing, the individual not only legitimates one view but delegitimates others.

But every way of seeing is also a way of not seeing; and in this case a view of man as essentially property-owning or self-interested or 'rational' or concerned to maximise his utility amounts to the ideological legitimation of a particular view of society and social relations – and the implicit delegitimation of others. (Lukes, 1973, pp. 149–50)

In relating this discussion to disability, it is not the ideological construction of property-owning, self-interested or rational individuals that is important. Rather it is the construction of 'able-bodied' and 'able-minded' individuals which is significant, with their physical capabilities of operating the new machines and their willingness to submit to the new work disciplines imposed by the factory.

This particular ideological construction can best be understood within Gramsci's distinction between 'organic' and 'arbitrary' ideologies.

> One must distinguish between historically organic ideologies, those, that is, which are necessary to a given structure, and ideologies that are arbitrary, rationalistic, or 'willed'. To the extent that ideologies are historically necessary they have a validity which is 'psychological'; they 'organise' human masses, and create the terrain on which men move, acquire consciousness of their position, struggle, etc. To the extent that they are arbitrary they only create individual 'movements', polemics and so on. (Gramsci, 1971, p. 377)

These organic and arbitrary ideologies, would better be called 'core' and 'peripheral', precisely because they are interrelated and interdependent; in this particular case the core (organic) ideology of individualism gives rise to the ideological construction of the disabled individual as the antithesis of able-bodiedness and able-mindedness, and the medicalisation of disability as a particular kind of problem. Precisely how this construction occurred now needs to be discussed.

THE INDIVIDUALISATION AND MEDICALISATION OF DISABILITY

How disability came to be conceived within the core ideology of individualism as an individual problem, can be understood by reference to the work of Foucault in general and his work on madness in particular (Foucault, 1965). His views have been summarised as follows:

> The very idea that 'madness' is individual pathology, a negative phenomenon, a defect to be remedied, is the object of his investigation. This concept of madness is not the achievement of psychiatric rationality. Rather it is a complex and non-intentional

social product, which formed the basis for psychiatry. (Hirst and Woolley, 1982, p. 165)

Thus, for Foucault, psychiatry as organised professional activity only becomes possible when (i) madness has been transformed from a diverse set of social valuations to a uniform category of pathology, and (ii) the mad have been excluded from normal social life and isolated in a specialist domain. Central to the argument is that there can be no such thing as madness without the idea of 'unmadness'; reason without unreason, to be less clumsy.

If we pursue this in relation to disability, then perhaps things will become clearer. The idea of disability as individual pathology only becomes possible when we have an idea of individual able-bodiedness, which is itself related to the rise of capitalism and the development of wage labour. Prior to this, the individual's contribution had been to the family, the community, the band, in terms of labour, and while, of course differences in individual contributions were noted, and often sanctions applied, individuals did not, in the main, suffer exclusion. Under capitalism that is precisely what happened and disability became individual pathology; disabled people could not meet the demands of individual wage labour and so became controlled through exclusion.

This process of exclusion was facilitated by focusing on the body, of individuals and populations, and with the rise of capitalism, the main group who came to focus their gaze on the body, was the medical profession. As disabled people were part of the process of control by exclusion, the medicalising of disability was connected to the rise of the medical profession and the development of 'the germ theory of illness and disease'.

A classic illustration of the medical model is the germ theory, derived from the scientific medical work of Pasteur and Koch in the nineteenth century; their work established a scientific basis for the emergence of medicine as a profession equipped with a satisfactory knowledge basis. The medical model is not concerned primarily with questions of prevention since it approaches the problem of disease through the experience of germ theory which involves a highly interventionist and specific form of medical practice. Germ theory was simply one component within a wider scientific revolution in Victorian medicine. (Turner, 1987, p. 214)

This approach, based upon the medical model, ignores the experience of illness and disease and neglects issues of prevention. In addition many of the major disorders in modern society have no known biochemical cause or are unresponsive to medical treatments. Finally, this approach ignores the influence that cultural, or even sub-cultural factors, may have upon the disease process. Despite these well-known criticisms, it remains true that in the twentieth century, we have seen an increasing medicalisation of society; medicine has acquired the right to define and treat a whole range of conditions and problems that previously would have been regarded as moral or social in origin (Conrad and Schneider, 1980; Manning and Oliver, 1985).

That disability has become medicalised, there can be no doubt. Doctors are centrally involved in the lives of disabled people from the determination of whether a foetus is handicapped or not through to the deaths of old people from a variety of disabling conditions. Some of these involvements are, of course, entirely appropriate, as in the diagnosis of impairment, the stabilisation of medical condition after trauma, the treatment of illness occurring independent of disability and the provision of physical rehabilitation. But doctors are also involved in assessing driving ability, prescribing wheelchairs, determining the allocation of financial benefits, selecting educational provision and measuring work capabilities and potential; in none of these cases is it immediately obvious that medical training and qualifications make doctors the most appropriate persons to be so involved. Not only that, but many of the newer professions such as physiotherapy, occupational therapy, health visiting, nursing and even teaching, either work in organisations hierarchically dominated by doctors or have their professional practice structured by a discourse based upon the medical model.

There have, of course been substantial gains from this medicalisation of disability, which has increased survival rates and prolonged life expectancies for many disabled people as well as eradicating some disabling conditions. But the issue for the late twentieth century is not one of life-expectancy but expectation of life and it is here that the negative and partial view prompted by medicalisation is most open to criticism.

The medical model of disability is one rooted in an undue emphasis on clinical diagnosis, the very nature of which is destined to lead to a partial and inhibiting view of the disabled individual.

In order to understand disability as an experience, as a lived thing, we need much more than the medical 'facts', however necessary these are in determining medication. The problem comes when they determine not only the form of treatment (if treatment is appropriate), but also the form of life for the person who happens to be disabled. (Brisenden, 1986, p. 173)

The medicalisation of everyday life and of society is thus a fact for the vast majority of the current population, disabled people among them. How this general phenomenon came about now needs to be considered along with specific explanations of how the process occurred in respect of disability. To facilitate this, the historical framework developed by Abrams (1982) and discussed in the previous chapter, will be returned to, incorporating enlightenment, necessity, action and power theories of welfare.

THEORIES OF MEDICALISATION

The enlightenment theory of medicalisation suggests that medicalisation is a consequence of both the rise of science and the progress of humanitarian ideas. Within this explanation, medicalisation is seen as largely beneficial and progressive, providing treatment to the ill rather than physical punishment for sinners, or deprivation of liberty for the criminal. While this may appear to be progressive, treatment may not always be experienced in this light and the consequences of medical labels may be negative and profound. This point has been made with regard to epilepsy:

In the initial decades of this century much was learned about epilepsy. As a result physicians gained much better control of the epileptic process (which sometimes results in seizures). The desire to control the disease, however, seems to go hand in hand with the desire to control the diseased person. Thus, epileptics were both helped and harmed; they were benefitted insofar as their illness was more accurately diagnosed and better treated; they were injured insofar as they, as persons, were stigmatised and socially segregated ... It has taken decades of work, much of it still unfinished, to undo some of the oppressive social effects of 'medical progress' in epilepsy, and to restore the epileptic to the social status he enjoyed before his disease became so well understood. Paradoxically then, what is good for epilepsy may not be good for the epileptic. (Szasz, 1966, p. 3)

This leads on to the necessity theory of medicalisation, which stresses the need to impose order in the new industrial society and describes the way in which medicine became the main agent in this process of social control (Zola, 1972). This explanation contains two strands; one seeing medicine as an independent social and ideological force and the other seeing medicine as an agent of the capitalist ruling class and a contributor to the 'legitimation of capitalism' (Navarro, 1976). Allying medicalisation and social control has its drawbacks, for it has the potential to produce a system of social control 'unlimited in its potential applications' (Kittrie, 1971, p. 362); and a profession and society

which are so concerned with physical and functional well being as to sacrifice civil liberty and moral integrity must inevitably press for a scientific environment similar to that provided for laying hens on progressive chicken farms – hens who produce eggs industriously and have no disease or other cares. (Freidson, 1970, p. 356)

The action theory of medicalisation sees this process as the struggle between various groups to impose their own specific set of meanings upon particular social phenomena. Within this framework, the question of why medical labels stick to some groups or conditions and not others is always an empirical question. Hence campaigns to medicalise some conditions such as alcoholism and hyperkinesis and to demedicalise others such as homosexuality are always consequent upon the struggle between competing groups. The fact that throughout the twentieth century, far more social phenomena have been medicalised than demedicalised is explained by reference to the notion of 'medical imperialism', the medical profession winning battles both to define and treat these phenomena.

What it does not explain is the success of the medical profession in achieving this dominant position. This requires a further dimension, supplied by the power theory of medicalisation. There are at least three versions of this; the first suggests that this dominance has been achieved because of the superiority of medical knowledge (based on science) over other forms of knowledge; the second suggests that power was achieved because the medical profession was well-organised and able to gain dominant positions within the new bureaucracies arising as part of the rationalising of society; the third emphasises the interconnections between the medical profession and the capitalist ruling class.

These explanations, taken separately, offer only a partial account of the medicalisation process for it was certainly shaped by the development of scientific and medical knowledge, by the need for more effective and far-reaching forms of social control, by the struggles between competing groups and by the structure and location of power. What is needed is an explanation which incorporates all these elements; which reconceptualises medical intervention as social control, medical knowledge as ideology and which links the two. But before attempting to provide this kind of explanation, it needs to be noted that few writers have attempted to explain this issue of the medicalisation of disability.

While there is an ever-burgeoning literature on the medicalisation of social problems generally, there have been few attempts to discuss the medicalisation of disability, either in historical or current context. Where disability is discussed, its location within the medical model goes unchallenged and explanations for medically-dominated service provision rarely go beyond the enlightenment theory of welfare. There are two exceptions to this, however, which need to be discussed.

The first of these is contained in the work of Stone (1985) who casts doctors in the role of 'reluctant imperialists'. Her central thesis is that the disability category performs the function of sorting people into the work-based or needs-based systems, and consequently, some allocation method needed to be developed in order to carry out this task. This was done by making disability a clinical concept and hence, assigning the role of allocation to the medical profession. However,

disability certification was not a task the profession wanted to assume. Most physicians believed that medical science was not capable of assessing disability, and that adoption of the certifying role would only create enormous tensions between doctors and their patients. (Stone, 1985, p. 112)

However, once it became obvious that medical certification was going to be the mechanism of allocation, the profession took the role on, fearing that if they did not, a government-created corps of physicians might grow up to rival their own independent profession.

While it may be true that certain key members of the American Medical Association took this view at one time specifically in respect of disability, the medical profession as a whole has not been reluctantly imperialist in industrial societies, notably with regard to other areas such as madness. Hence the medicalisation of disability was as much a product of the structural position of the medical profession in capitalist society as it was the attitudes and beliefs of particular groups of doctors.

Just such a structural explanation has been provided by Finkelstein (1980) who links medicalisation with the rise of the institution and the segregation of disabled people and who argues that this segregation facilitated the development of a whole range of specialist, professional workers.

Thus the hospital environment facilitated the development of nurses, physiotherapists, occupational therapists, social workers (almoners), counsellors, etc., and the alms houses, asylums, charitable homes ensured the success of the move towards segregation. *The development of successful medical practices in hospitals ensured greater numbers of people with physical impairments surviving and must have strengthened the connection between disabled people and institutions as well as facilitating the medical dominance in the field.* (My emphasis; Finkelstein, 1980, p. 10)

But seeing medicalisation (medical dominance in Finkelstein's terms) arising from the establishment and success of hospital-based medicine is only part of the story, for this hospital-based medicine itself arose out of the need to classify and control the population and to distinguish between workers and non-workers within the new capitalist social order. Hence the medicalisation of disability occurred historically as part of this wider social process, and the strategic position that the medical profession was able to achieve for itself under capitalism.

Part of the reason for this medicalisation generally was the success of the germ-theory approach to treating certain conditions, but the twentieth century has seen some fundamental changes in the patterns of disease and disability.

> Changing patterns of disease and societal response to these new problems has aggravated the medical care crisis and underlined the growing importance of the disability problem. The health problems apparent today have few quick and inexpensive solutions. (Albrecht and Levy, 1984, p. 49)

Medical interventions based upon germ theory are no longer successful with the chronic and degenerative diseases which are coming to dominate morbidity rates in modern, industrial societies. There are no cures, and maintenance rather than treatment has come to play a major part in medical intervention.

This raises the question as to why, given this changing pattern and the fact that many disabling conditions no longer respond to medical treatments (i.e. the cure), does the medical profession continue to dominate the sphere of disability? A major factor, undoubtedly, is that the medical profession has expanded the area of its activity, to rehabilitation as well as treatment, as the pattern of diseases shifted from acute to chronic.

> As demand for rehabilitation services increased and insurance benefits expanded, there was an incentive for physicians to enter the rehabilitative field. Under the aegis of designing comprehensive medical rehabilitation programs, hospitals, and physicians began to incorporate rehabilitation services into the medical model. Definitions of disabling conditions and appropriate treatments were expanded to include medical intervention and physician control. (Albrecht and Levy, 1981, p. 22)

The power of the medical profession and its strategic structural position cannot mask the defects in the medicalisation of rehabilitation any more than they can mask the defects in the medicalisation of treatment.

These defects are well-known: the physicalist nature of its programmes to the neglect of other personal and social factors (Oliver *et al.*, 1988); the difficulties in measuring success or failure and hence the concentration on employment status as a measure of success (Albrecht and Levy, 1984); and the failure to involve disabled people meaningfully in the whole rehabilitation process (Finkelstein, 1988). Even the economic rationality underpinning the rehabilitation industry is being called into question; originally developed to turn (or return) people into productive and socially useful human beings, their cost-effectiveness is increasingly being called into question:

> Disability programs are considered to be very expensive and rapidly becoming more so, and there is concern whether resources are being efficiently allocated. (Erlanger and Roth, 1985, p. 319)

CORE AND PERIPHERAL IDEOLOGIES

Despite these criticisms and questions, the medical and rehabilitation enterprises remain two of the most important of the human service industries and this is closely connected with the way both practices are linked to social control and their theories fit with the ideology of capitalism and the construction of the able-bodied individual. Thus, for example,

> The aim of returning the individual to normality is the central foundation stone upon which the whole rehabilitation machine is constructed. If, as happened to me following my spinal injury, the disability cannot be cured, normative assumptions are not abandoned. On the contrary, they are re-formulated so that they not only dominate the treatment phase searching for a cure but also totally colour the helper's perception of the rest of that person's life. The rehabilitation aim now becomes to assist the individual to be as 'normal as possible'.
>
> The result, for me, was endless soul-destroying hours at Stoke Mandeville Hospital trying to approximate to able-bodied standards by 'walking' with calipers and crutches... Rehabilitation philosophy emphasises physical normality and, with this, the attainment of skills that allow the individual to approximate as closely as possible to able-bodied behaviour (e.g. only using a wheelchair as a last resort, rather than seeing it as a disabled peoples' mobility aid like a pair of shoes is an able-bodied person's mobility aid). (Finkelstein, 1988, pp. 4–5)

This ideology of able-bodied normality underpins the professional approach to the issue of disability from pre-birth until death. Thus, the Abortion Act (1967) makes termination possible if 'there is a substantial risk that if the child were born it would suffer from such physical or mental abnormalities as to be seriously handicapped'. No strict criteria are laid down to specify abnormality, nor is a definition of seriously handicapped provided, so the termination decision is left in the hands of two doctors. Given the earlier discussion of the difficulties of defining disability and handicap, this decision will ultimately be based upon personal judgements of individuals, who, whatever their training, are not immune from the fetters of the ideology of the able-bodied and able-minded individual.

It should be made clear that this is not an attempt to engage in the 'abortion debate' but to illustrate the similarities in the ideologies of professional practice in otherwise disparate areas. This ideology underpinning abortion has implications for disabled people:

> The general consensus is that if a disabled person admits that eugenic abortion is justifiable, he is thereby undermining the value of his own life. (Graham Monteith, 1987, p. 38)

and for society:

> if able-bodied society were to accept that those with disabilities are equal human beings with rights, they would also have to abandon the notion that screening and abortion are benefits to society, and that the earlier a handicapped person is killed off the better for all concerned. (Davis, 1987, p. 287)

This ideology is not only relevant to life-and-death issues but to other areas as well. The current popularity of 'conductive education' is a product of this ideology of the able-bodied individual, for its aim is to teach children with cerebral palsy to walk, talk and engage in all other activities in as near normal a way as possible. No consideration is given to the issue of the ideology of 'normality' nor to the idea that the environment could be changed rather than the individual.

> The object of Conductive Education is not to accommodate the severe dysfunctional patients in an institute, or to send them to a

special school, but to accomplish a basic task to render possible a normal education, travelling in the streets, self-supporting and work. In order to bring about an equilibrium between child and environment, we do not change the environment, but the adaptation of the child's constitution. (Hari, 1968, quoted in Cottam and Sutton, 1985, pp. 41–2)

And scant regard is paid to the costs involved in terms of pain, coercion, loss of childhood, disruption of family life, acceptance of alternative ways of doing things, and so on. Again this is not a consideration of the pros and cons of conductive education but a pointer to the ideological similarities that it has with other practices.

The search for the cure of a variety of disabling conditions such as multiple sclerosis, muscular dystrophy and spinal injury is also supported by this ideology as is much of the practice of geriatric medicine aimed at restoring the functional capacities of old people rather than providing the support of services which allow them to live in dignity with their declining physical capabilities. Long ago, the unitary idea of able-bodied and able-mindedness was mocked:

in an important sense there is only one complete unblushing male in America: a young, married, white, heterosexual Protestant father of college education, fully employed, of good complexion, weight and height, and a recent record in sports ... The general identity values of a society may be fully entrenched nowhere, and yet they can cast some kind of shadow on the encounters encountered everywhere in daily living. (Goffman, 1963, pp. 128–9)

But these identity values can be structurally located and are fully entrenched in the core ideology of individualism and they cast a shadow on the lives of disabled people through their incorporation into the peripheral ideologies of able-bodiedness and able-mindedness and the medicalisation of disability.

Shadows are cast on the lives of disabled people not simply because of the existence of these ideologies but because of the discursive practices (Foucault, 1972) which accompany them. Hence, if we return to the issue of the cure for disabling conditions, the discursive practices surrounding this issue usually focus on walking. Ignoring the strictures of Finkelstein (1988) on walking, Dr Hari suggests

The duty of the pedagogue is to promote the discovery of conditions which enable the spinal cord injury patient to learn how to walk, etc. and enter everyday life without any special mechanism.

But further, 'In order to make a spinal cord injury patient walk, teaching must restore the will of the individual to do so. (Hari, 1975, quoted in Cottam and Sutton, 1985, pp. 161–2) Thus the implication is clear: those who remain unable to walk, lack the will so to do.

Similarly, in respect of ageing, much medical intervention is geared towards returning the old person to as near normality as possible. Usually the spoken assumptions behind this normality are the functional capacities and capabilities of twenty-five-year-olds and it is these to which the old person must aspire. Further

The bio-medical theories not only individualise and medicalise old age, but also they overlook the relationship between socio-economic status, the economy and health. (Estes *et al.*, 1982, p. 153)

This has further consequences in that it is becoming increasingly less possible

to debate the broad span of social and allied policies necessary to change the attitudes which exist in this political and cultural climate which identifies older people as patients and social casualties. (Midwinter, 1987, p. 1234)

Shapiro (1981) uses this idea to discuss stuttering as disability and suggests that these discursive practices direct our attention to the stutterer's mouth as the source of the problem of stuttering. He goes on to suggest there are, however, other choices on which we could focus our attention.

In the case of the stuttering child, for example, one might well ignore the mouth and deal with the parent–child relationship, for the parents might be putting pressure on the child that, if removed, might bring an end to stuttering. Or, going further out in the causal sequence, the parents might be under pressure, given such situations as a stressful work setting or a stressful marital relationship. (Shapiro, 1981, pp. 92–3)

He goes on to suggest that we could move further and further away from the stutterer's mouth until we focused on the 'structure of the economy as a whole'.

But his analysis itself remains locked into a discursive practice which sees stuttering as stress-related. An alternative might be to see stuttering as merely a natural phenomenon and one of the myriad ways in which communication takes place, which might also include Oxbridge English, Esperanto, sign language, Braille, Makaton and so on. Thus the problem of stuttering can therefore be seen as the result of social expectations about appropriate (and inappropriate) ways of communicating rather than the product of stress among individuals or families.

Shapiro, of course, recognises that these discursive practices are not free-floating but grounded in particular concrete practices and forms of social relations. And

The way that we speak about phenomena like stuttering is conditioned by the discourses within which such phenomena are embedded. Speech pathology, for example, is not a phenomenon lying around waiting to be discovered. It is an ideological commitment that represents various modes of responsibility and control. The fact that 'speech problems' are regarded as such is thus the function of a latent ideology, one that is structurally represented by the vocations of persons such as speech therapists. We therefore look into the mouths of stutterers because we regard it as relatively more legitimate to load the responsibility for stuttering onto the stutterer than elsewhere. (Shapiro, 1981, p. 93)

Hence disability is structurally represented by the vocations of doctors and the para-medical professions, and we load responsibility for the restrictions that disabled people experience on to disabled people themselves, who are restricted because of the functional or psychological limitations imposed by their individual impairments rather than by the social restrictions imposed by society.

To sum up, the disabled individual is an ideological construction related to the core ideology of individualism and the peripheral ideologies related to medicalisation and normality. And the individual experience of disability is structured by the discursive practices which stem from these ideologies.

Lukes, in his discussion of individualism in general, comes to conclusions of relevance to the ideological construction of the disabled individual. He recognises that there have been indispensible gains from the rise of individualism; it was central to the breaking down of traditional hierarchies and privileges and in establishing the legal rights of individuals. Further, he suggests that

> These are crucial and indispensible gains but, if we are to take equality and liberty seriously, they must be transcended. *And that can only be achieved on the basis of a view of un-abstracted individuals in their concrete, social specificity, who in virtue of being persons, all require to be treated and to live in a social order which treats them as possessing dignity, as capable of exercising and increasing their autonomy, of engaging in valued activities within a private space, and of developing their several potentialities.* (My emphasis; Lukes, 1973, p. 153)

Likewise, this is not to deny the real and indispensible gains brought about by the individualisation and medicalisation of disability, but these gains must also be transcended and the italicised portion of the above quotation would not be out of place in any charter on disability. Before considering the implications of this view of un-abstracted individuals for disability policy, it is necessary to consider the disabled individual who is located within this ideological construction, and that will be discussed in the following chapter.

5

The Structuring of Disabled Identities

The personal response of individuals to their disabilities cannot be understood merely as a reaction to trauma or tragedy but have to be located within a framework which takes account of both history and ideology. Thus

> a materialist understanding of the individual must centre upon two aspects of the ensemble of social relations of which the person is constituted: the performance of labour and the incorporation of ideology. (Leonard, 1984, p. 180)

The effects of changes in the labour market and their implications for social relations have already been discussed in Chapter 3, and the incorporation of the ideology of individualism has been described in Chapter 4; the effects that these factors have on identity formation for disabled people will be discussed below.

There is no doubt that the historical process has a significant influence on identity formation in general, for

> there is a considerable consensus about the extent to which the process must be seen as a matter of a specifically historical entry into some specific historical figuration – an interweaving of personal and collective histories. In this double sense identity formation en masse is seen as a historically located historical sequence. (Abrams, 1982, p. 241)

This 'historically located historical sequence' implies that there is a cultural context to identity formation, and as far as disability is concerned raises the question as to whether there is a culture of disability.

CULTURE AND DISABILITY

Earlier it was suggested that prior to the rise of capitalism, disabled people were integrated within their communities and had a legitimated number of social (and economic) roles. Their exclusion as a consequence of the rise of capitalism had an influence on this cultural context as an analysis of the presentation of disability in the Victorian novel suggests.

Not until the rise of sentimentalism and the obsession with the excluded and the marginal, which climaxes in the reign of Victoria, did the blind, the deaf and the halt become major characters in large numbers of books written by authors and intended for readers who, thinking of themselves as non-handicapped, are able to regard the handicapped as essentially alien, absolute others. In such a context, fellow human beings with drastically impaired perception, manipulation and ambulation tend, of course, to be stereotyped, either negatively or positively; but in any case rendered as something more or less than human. (Fiedler, 1981)

Throughout the twentieth century, whether it be in the novel, newspaper stories or television and films, disabled people continue to be portrayed as more than or less than human, rarely as ordinary people doing ordinary things. Without a full analysis of images of disability it is not possible to do other than present examples of these images. Sir Clifford, in *Lady Chatterley's Lover*, is an obvious example of the presentation of disabled people as less than human. The story of Sir Douglas Bader as portrayed in *Reach For The Sky* is an example of a disabled person being portrayed as more than human. These portrayals see disabled people either as pathetic victims of some appalling tragedy or as superheroes struggling to overcome a tremendous burden. But the image of disabled people as more than human does not always emphasise goodness, for as a recent analysis of children's fiction has shown

the disabled adult has often been portrayed as an embittered and menacing character who, like Long John Silver, seeks to manipulate children for his own ends, or as a man bearing a grudge against society, who uses his distorted body or artificial limbs in a sinister and aggressive fashion, e.g. Captain Hook. (Quicke, 1985 p. 122)

In recent years there has been a growing recognition of the fact that these dominant cultural images not only violate the actual experience of disability, but also are positively unhelpful in providing role models for disabled people and in breaking down prejudice amongst the rest of the population. Thus there have been attempts, particularly by the mass media, to break down some of these images through the development of specialist programmes, drama and documentaries, but there is still a long way to go; at present, the best that can be said is that dominant images are being challenged but they are far from being replaced by more authentic ones. The disability arts movement is increasingly becoming the focus of the mounting of these challenges but it has, itself, had to struggle to free itself from the domination of able-bodied professionals who tended to stress arts as therapy (Lord, 1981) rather than arts as cultural imagery. That, too, is changing, for as disabled people struggle to take control over their own lives,

The same process has been happening in the arts. Disabled people who were active in the arts are increasingly meeting with those who were active in what might be called, the politics of disability, and together we are trying to develop a new way of looking at, and presenting, disability 'as a way of life'. (Finkelstein, 1987, p. 1)

The point about this brief discussion of cultural images has been to show how they support the ideology of individualism, in presenting the disabled individual as less than or more than human. There has been little attempt to present the collective experience of disability culturally, and hence the process of identity formation for disabled individuals has usually been constrained by images of superheroes or pathetic victims. But this process of identity formation does not merely take place within the context of what Mead (1934) might have called 'the generalised other' but of 'significant others' as well. Crucial significant others in the lives of disabled people are those vast array of professionals who either write things about or do things to disabled people. Their world-views of disability, heavily influenced by the medical profession, also individualise disability and reinforce the less than human cultural image of disabled people. It is the effects of this on disability identity formation which will next be considered.

ADJUSTMENT – A PSYCHOLOGICAL APPROACH

In Gramsci's terms these significant others are 'intellectuals', though he gives this term a broad meaning.

> By 'intellectuals' must be understood not those strata commonly described by this term, but in general the entire social stratum which exercises an organisational function in the wide sense – whether in the field of production, or in that of culture, or in that of political administration. (Gramsci, 1971, p. 97)

In terms of disability, these intellectuals are precisely that group of people who do things to or write things about disabled people and both their theories and their practice are constrained by the ideology of individualism and by cultural images of disabled people as less than human.

The concept which links these strands is that of adjustment. The argument suggests that when something happens to an individual's body something happens to the mind as well. Thus, in order to become fully human again, in order to form a disabled identity, the disabled individual must undergo medical treatment and physical rehabilitation (see the previous chapter) as well as the process of psychological adjustment or coming to terms with disability. Further, in order to adjust satisfactorily, the individual may need to grieve and mourn for his lost ability and pass through a series of stages before adjustment is complete.

However, the conceptual framework provided by the adjustment has been severely criticised on theoretical grounds (Finkelstein, 1980; Oliver, 1981) as well as on the grounds that it does not accord with the actual experience of disability (Sutherland, 1981), and alternative frameworks such as social adjustment (Oliver *et al.*, 1988) and social oppression (UPIAS, 1976) have been developed. But it is not just disabled people who have provided theoretical and experiential criticisms of this framework, but researchers also have found it difficult to provide empirical evidence.

Our view of the available literature suggests that a great deal of variability exists in individual reactions to negative life events, both within a particular life crisis and across different crises. We have found little reliable evidence to indicate that people go through stages of emotional responses following an undesirable life event. We have also reviewed a substantial body of evidence suggesting that a large minority of victims of aversive life events experience distress or disorganisation long after recovery might be expected. Current theoretical models of reactions to aversive outcomes cannot account for the variety of responses that appear. (Silver and Wortman, 1980, p. 309)

The crucial issue this raises is why does the concept of adjustment exert such a powerful influence over what professionals (intellectuals) actually say and do about disability? It is clear that this influence cannot be accounted for in terms of theoretical coherence or empirical grounding, for as one disabled sociologist has pointed out in reflecting upon his own experience of disability,

I realised how meager are our attempts to write and do research about adjustment and adaptation. It would be nice if, at some point, growing up ends and maturity begins, or if one could say that successful adjustment and adaptation to a particular difficulty has been achieved. For most problems, or perhaps most basic life issues, there is no single time for such a resolution to occur. The problems must be faced, evaluated, re-defined, and readapted to, again and again and again. And I knew now that this applied to myself. No matter how much I was admired by others or by myself, there was still much more I had to face. 'My Polio' and 'My Accident' were not just my past; they were part of my present and my future. (Zola, 1982, p. 84)

Hence, professionals are clearly influenced by cultural images and ideological constructions of disability as an individual, medical and tragic problem. The issue of adjustment, therefore, became the focus for professional intervention and reinforced these very images and constructions by rooting them in practice.

In recent years a link has emerged between these professional constructions of disability as adjustment and cultural images of disabled people. Hence,

The most prevalent image in films and especially in television during the past several decades has been the maladjusted disabled person. These stories involve characters with physical or sensory, rather than mental handicaps. The plots follow a consistent pattern: The disabled central characters are bitter and self-pitying because, however long they have been disabled, they have never adjusted to their handicaps, and never accepted themselves as they are. (Longmore, 1987, p. 70)

Thus, it is disabled people who have the problem. They treat their families and friends badly until long-suffering enough, they confront these disabled people giving them 'an emotional slap in the face'. The disabled person then realises that it is him or her who has the problem, accepts the rebuke and becomes a well-adjusted adult.

The problems with these cultural images, as with professional constructions, is that they ignore issues of social prejudice and institutional discrimination. The non-disabled have little trouble in accepting disabled people and indeed understand the problems of disability better than the disabled people themselves. Thus, ultimately these images place 'responsibility for any problems squarely and almost exclusively on the disabled individual' (Longmore, 1987, p. 71)

STIGMA – A SOCIAL PSYCHOLOGICAL APPROACH

A significant advance on the purely psychological conceptions of adjustment is the idea of stigma, originally advanced in the work of Goffman (1963). He pointed out that stigmas were originally inflicted, through marking or branding, on certain individuals who had transgressed the norms or values of a particular society. In modern societies stigmas emerged through the processes of social interaction whereby individuals were marked out or set aside because of some attribute they possessed or because something discreditable was known about them. Stigmatised identities were formed through interpersonal interactions rather than psychological reactions to events. Thus while stigma may have existed in all societies, in ancient ones it was inflicted because of some transgression or other; in modern societies, the stigma itself was the transgression. In both kinds of societies, stigma implied moral opprobrium or blameworthiness.

Partly because of Goffman's position in social science, and partly because of the originality of his insights, stigma became the dominant conceptual framework for developing an understanding of the experience of disability. No one mentioned that the empirical evidence for his insights was derived from secondary sources heavily dominated by psychological models (Barker *et al.*, 1953; Wright, 1960) and that much of this data was gathered in one country in one specific period. And only Finkelstein (1980) pointed out that while Goffman's work was concerned with social contexts, interactions and processes, stigma was ultimately reducible to the individual; there could be no stigmatising process unless the individual possessed a stigma in the first place.

There were some attempts at implicit criticism when Goffman's framework didn't quite match empirical reality, and it therefore needed to be extended and developed to understand the stigma of homosexuality (Humphreys, 1972) or leprosy (Gussow and Tracey, 1968):

> he deals mainly with single individuals in brief encounters with normals, usually in 'unfocussed gatherings'. He seems less concerned with patients' efforts towards destigmatisation in more permanent groupings, especially in social settings where they live together in more or less continuous interaction, where they are able to develop their own subculture, norms and ideology, and where they possess some measure of control over penetrating dissonant and discrediting views from without. (Gussow and Tracy, 1968, p. 316)

Thus, while stigma may be an appropriate metaphor for describing what happens to individual disabled people in social interactions, it is unable to explain why this stigmatisation occurs or to incorporate collective rather than personal responses to stigma.

A recent attempt has been made to rescue stigma from its individualistic, interactionist and relativist position (Ainley *et al.*, 1986) almost to the point of providing a sociological account.

> The overall structure of society is determined not only by its cultural attributes such as norms, values and religious beliefs but also by the nature of its social organisations and its political and economic structures. These factors contribute significantly to the

way in which the concept of stigma is used and how it is viewed in society. (Becker and Arnold, 1986 p. 44)

Unfortunately, while this is acknowledged, stigma is still reduced to individual adaptation.

Changing one's appearance is one of many ways to cope with stigma. For most persons with visible stigmas, however, such a change is not possible. For these persons – ethnic minorities and those with physical disabilities – and for all the persons with 'hidden stigmas', coping with stigma is a process of individual adaptation. (Becker and Arnold, 1986, pp. 49–50)

The idea that individuals might confront, reject, or ignore, as a deliberate strategy, their stigmas rather than cope with them, is not even considered. Stigma is all embracing but still an individual problem.

And even when considering the political movement of disabled people, it is analysed in terms of destigmatisation and interactional processes.

At one time almost totally isolated from the general population, disabled people are today more visible and often live in the mainstream of American society. One purpose of this social movement has been to look beyond the particulars of specific disabilities to the commonalities experienced by all disabled people and their experience of stigma. Consequently, some of the stigma attached to physically disabled as a group has lessened, and individual self-esteem has improved as well. (Becker and Arnold, 1986, pp. 54–5)

Thus the political movement of disabled people is seen as synonymous with the self-help movement; populist and the more explicitly political aspects of the movement are ignored.

Within the book, the consideration of the issue of social control offers the opportunity to provide a structural account of stigma but again this is not taken, for

Social control involves reactions to stigmas (or deviance). Reactions may occur for various reasons (e.g. fear, vengeance), but an important consequence is often the restriction or termination of social relations. (Stafford and Scott, 1986, p. 87)

Stafford and Scott do not mean social relations in the sociological sense of the term, however, but interpersonal relations, as with skinny children being excluded from neighbourhood games of basketball, and the avoidance of ugly people as dating partners. No mention of the exclusion of disabled people in segregated institutions as part of the process of social control is even acknowledged.

Thus, disabled people have not found stigma a helpful or useful concept in developing and formulating their own collective experience of disability as social restriction. To begin with, it has been unable (so far) to throw off the shackles of the individualistic approach to disability with its focus on the discredited and the discreditable. In addition, its focus on process and interpersonal interactions ignores the institutionalised practices ingrained with social relations (in the sociological sense). And finally, therefore, they have preferred to reinterpret the collective experiences in terms of structural notions of discrimination and oppression rather than interpersonal ones of stigma and stigmatisation.

SOCIAL ADJUSTMENT – A SOCIOLOGICAL APPROACH

Thus, neither the psychological nor the social-psychological approaches provides an adequate account of the experience of disability and, as has already been mentioned, there have been attempts to develop alternative frameworks using the concepts of social adjustment and social oppression. These attempt to locate the experience of disability within a wider social context and to consider the wider social forces which structure the experience of disability.

In a study of the experience of spinal cord injury, the concept of social adjustment was developed to facilitate an understanding of the wide variety of personal responses to spinal injury:

understanding the consequences of SCI involves a complex relationship between the impaired individual, the social context within which the impairment occurs and the meanings available to individuals to enable them to make sense of what is happening. This is what we mean by social adjustment: it is more than simply

the functional limitations that an individual has or the social restrictions encountered; it is a complex relationship between impairment,
social restrictions and meaning. (Oliver *et al.*, 1988, pp. 11–12)

The experience of spinal injury, therefore, cannot be understood
in terms of purely internal psychological or interpersonal processes,
but requires a whole range of other material factors such as housing,
finance, employment, the built environment and family circumstances
to be taken into account. Further, all of these material factors can
and will change over time, sometimes for the better and sometimes
for the worse, hence giving the experience of disability a temporal
dimension. This framework does not need to present disabled people
as more than or less than human but rather as 'ordinary people
coping with extraordinary circumstances'. While this is a significant
advance, the study does concentrate on one type of impairment and
does not attempt to show how these material factors are related to
wider social forces.

The idea that disability was a particular form of social oppression
was first articulated by the Union of the Physically Impaired
Against Segregation in 1975; subsequently it was used by a group of
disabled people to analyse their own experiences of disability
(Sutherland, 1981); and later, incorporated within a materialist
framework (Leonard, 1984). However, to analyse disability as
oppression from an experiential base is not itself enough, for

To claim that disabled people are oppressed involves . . . arguing a
number of other points. At an empirical level, it is to argue that on
significant dimensions disabled people can be regarded as a group
whose members are in an inferior position to other members of
society because they are disabled people. It is also to argue that
these disadvantages are dialectically related to an ideology or
group of ideologies which justify and perpetuate this situation.
Beyond this it is to make the claim that such disadvantages and
their supporting ideologies are neither natural nor inevitable.
Finally it involves the identification of some beneficiary of this
state of affairs. (Abberley, 1987, p. 7)

As Abberley himself acknowledges, there is plenty of empirical
evidence to suggest that disabled people are in an inferior position,
whether it be in terms of housing (Borsay, 1986a), employment

(Lonsdale, 1986), finance (Townsend, 1979), transport (Hoad, 1986) or education (Anderson, 1979). That these disadvantages are related to the core ideology of individualism and the peripheral ideologies underpinning medicalisation and personal tragedy theory was the argument presented in the previous chapter. Chapter 2 provided examples to show that disabled people are not treated as inferior in all societies nor at all historical points, thus demonstrating that their supporting ideologies are neither natural nor inevitable. Finally, the broad answer to the question 'Who benefits?', is that capitalism itself benefits in that disabled people may perform an economic function as part of the reserve pool of labour and an ideological function in being maintained in their position of inferiority. Thus they serve as a warning to those unable or unwilling to work (Oliver, 1986).

It is clear from this that disability can be seen both objectively and subjectively as a particular form of oppression. But again, as Abberley points out, this is not to suggest that a monolithic theory of oppression, into which all oppressed groups are fitted, can be developed. Disability is a particular form of oppression, in that sexual and racial oppression are 'wholly ideological'; whereas impairment is 'real' and 'forms a bedrock upon which justificatory oppressive theories are based' (Abberley, 1987, p. 8). This oppression is also multi-dimensional rather than monolithic in that 'more than half the disabled people in Britain today suffer the additional burden of racial and/or sexual oppression' (Abberley, 1987, p. 7). It is to the ways that experience of disability is structured in terms of race and gender that attention now needs to be focused.

WOMEN AND DISABILITY

While a great deal of material has been published on both specific impairments and disability in general, there has been almost no consideration of the ways in which gender might structure the experience of disability and hence disabled identities. To be sure some studies have discussed the experience of women as well as men (Blaxter, 1980; Sutherland, 1981) and one collection concentrated exclusively on the experience of women (Campling, 1981), but even there, few of the women specifically discussed the effects of gender on their experience of disability. Some national organisations, like the Spinal Injuries Association and the British Council of Organisations of Disabled People, have established groups to consider this issue, and internationally, Disabled People's International is currently sponsoring a similar initiative. But, as a recent American publication devoted specifically to an analysis of gender and disability, notes,

> Despite the attention given to disability in general and certain impairments in particular, one category within the disabled population has received little recognition or study: women. Like many social change movements, the disability movement has often directed its energies toward primarily male experiences. Male sexual concerns and employment issues, for example, have received more attention than child-bearing problems. (Deegan and Brooks, 1985, p. 1)

Part of the reason for this is that the experience of disability, like experience generally, is structured by the 'ideology of masculinity' (Brittan and Maynard, 1984), which limits the range of personal responses open to both disabled men and women.

> Whereas disabled men are obliged to fight the social stigma of disability, they can aspire to fill socially powerful male roles. Disabled women do not have this option. Disabled women are perceived as inadequate for economically productive roles (traditionally considered appropriate for males) and for the nurturant, reproductive roles considered appropriate for females. (Fine and Asch, 1985, p. 6)

Hence disabled women find it difficult to enter male roles but, at the same time are often denied access to traditional female roles because they are often seen as asexual and unsuitable for, or incapable of, motherhood.

It is this 'double disability' which structures the experience of disabled women and compounds the oppression of disability alone.

The lack of approved social roles for disabled women derives from a constellation of confounding forces. Disabled women (like racial or ethnic minority women) experience a major disadvantage in relation to their relevant 'single' minority reference groups:

disabled men and non-disabled women. The disadvantage is 'double' because disabled women fare worse than both relevant comparison groups economically, socially and psychologically. (Fine and Asch, 1985, p. 7)

While, from a theoretical (and political) point of view, this would certainly appear to be the case, there is a lack of substantive empirical data of either an objective or subjective kind which directly compares the experience of disabled women and men.

This can lead to an alternative position, albeit from a male viewpoint (Murphy, 1987), which suggests that the experience of disabled women may be less oppressive than that of disabled men. These arguments are now unknown to disabled women, who are happy to rehearse them without agreeing with them.

For example, it has long been thought that women's roles in society are not as severely limited by the wheelchair as are men's roles. The traditional view of sex roles holds that dependency and passivity are more natural for females than for males. A woman, even if disability requires that she use a wheelchair, can still manage a household, direct others in household tasks, provide emotional support to a family, and function sexually in a 'relatively passive' manner. (Bonwich, 1985, p. 56)

In other words, there are strong links between the assumed passivity of disabled people and the assumed passivity of women.

It should be recognised that this passivity associated with disabled people is not natural but 'wholly ideological' in Abberley's (1987) sense of the term. In the case of differences between disabled men and disabled women, even where these differences may appear to be 'real' or natural, this may not be the case. For example, the management of bladder incontinence, which is often assumed to be much more difficult for women than men, is usually explained in terms of biological differences. But surely biology cannot account for the vast array of methods, devices and equipment available to disabled men whereas disabled women only have the choice between catheterisation and incontinence pads? Even where new techniques such as the electro-stimulation of bladder muscles through surgical implants have been developed, considerably more have been given to men, who need them less, than women, who need them more.

Perhaps an appropriate slogan would be that 'incontinence is a feminist issue'.

Thus the different (and more oppressive) experience of disability for women does not occur naturally but because

> The combined forces of a hostile economy, a discriminatory society, and a negative self-image contribute to a systematic rolelessness for disabled women. There is no avenue for self-affirmation. (Fine and Asch, 1985, p. 9)

BLACK PEOPLE AND DISABILITY

There is a similar paucity of empirical material on the ways in which race may structure the individual and collective experiences of disability and hence its implications for disabled identity, although this issue is now beginning to be addressed. However, it has been argued that black, disabled identity can only be understood within the context of institutionalised racism which is defined as follows;

> 'All attitudes, procedures and patterns – social and economic – whose effect, though not necessarily whose conscious attention, is to create and maintain the power, influence and well-being of white people at the expense of black people.'
> Or, in other words ... the able-bodied have now become white and the disabled people black. It therefore follows that the black or Asian disabled person faces a double disadvantage: that of being both black and disabled. (Confederation of Indian Organisations, 1987, p. 2)

The crucial issue this raises is the double disadvantage of being both black and disabled.

Few studies have addressed this issue of double disadvantage, though it has been pointed out that current community care policies in Britain fail to consider the individual needs of black, disabled people (Connelly, 1988) and an American study has shown that black people fare considerably worse in obtaining disability benefits than do their white counterparts (Thorpe and Toikka, 1980). Similarly

> there is the suggestion that a handicapped person's race is a factor

in the decision making and will determine the rehabilitative services provided. The implication of the services provided is that whites are more likely than blacks to be self-sufficient after rehabilitation. (Baldwin and Smith, 1984, p. 313)

Thus amid a growing awareness that this problem exists, more research is being undertaken and calls are being made for more appropriate responses.

The findings of the research project so far make it clear that there is an urgent need to educate all members of the community about the needs of Afro-Caribbean disabled people. There needs to be more awareness about the disadvantages they face as a first step towards responding positively and appropriately towards them. This will only come about if Afro-Caribbean disabled people themselves are encouraged to communicate their needs, aspirations and expectations and suggest how best society can respond to them. (Nathwani, 1987, p. 15)

The record of voluntary organisations in dealing with issues of race is a poor one (NCVO, 1984), although some disability organisations, notably the Greater London Association of Disabled People, are beginning to address this issue, as other disability organisations are beginning to address the issue of gender. And specifically in respect of sickle cell disease, black people have begun to create their own organisations both to promote self-help and a better understanding of the disease as well as reducing the stigma attached to it. Further, they are beginning to move beyond stigma avoidance and are attempting to focus on service provision and more specifically political issues.

A recent conference has identified some of the key factors which structure the experience of being both black and disabled (Confederation of Indian Organisations, 1987, pp. 7–8):

1 Asian people's experience of disabilities are essentially different from other people with disabilities because of language difficulties and institutional racism.
2 There appears to be a severe lack of accessible information regarding available services, such as employment, education, training, recreation, grants and allowances for disabled people.

3   There is a need for Asian disabled people as well as their carers to meet one another and also integrate with the rest of the community: to combat the isolation that a lot of them experience and to do away with any stigma that may be attached to disability.

Clearly, then, race can have a considerable influence on identity formation in a similar way to gender, but if the evidence on the precise nature of this influence is slender in terms of race and gender separately, it is almost non-existent in terms of the ways in which being both black and female might structure the experience of disability.

RACE AND GENDER AND DISABILITY

One study which examined these issues found that

> Black men and white men were most similar in the losses they perceived, emphasising – more than the female subjects – loss of independence and inability to make and spend money. Women, on the other hand, were more concerned than were men with the effects of their disability on their personal relationships and responsibilities. Thus, losses attributed to disability seemed to be rather closely linked to societal sex role prescriptions. At the same time, inability to perform tasks, whether in the occupational sphere or inside the home, was the loss most frequently cited by all 4 race-sex groups, highlighting a need for effective vocational rehabilitation. (Kutner, 1979, p. 65)

This would suggest that the effects of disability on economic and gender-related roles are likely to have a more significant effect on the experience of disability than race, but on the basis of one study, this cannot be taken as definitive.

In the absence of empirical data, there has also been little theorising on the effects of a combination of race, gender and disability on personal experience, though it has been suggested that concepts like 'multiple minority statuses' and 'multiple minority groups' might be a useful starting point for analysis (Deegan, 1985). Not only might such concepts be a useful basis for generating an understanding of individual experiences but they may also have implications for a wider understanding of the way society functions, not as a massive united and anonymous force but as a complex and contradictory set of social relations. This also has implications for the way minority groups are perceived.

Instead of defining each minority as oppressed and restricted in opportunities by a large and unified majority, the pattern of such discrimination can be perceived as benefitting only a very small elite. This numerically tiny group benefits from the competition between disadvantaged groups. The dispossessed and second class citizens, because of their alienation and sense of isolation, allow themselves to be defined as in opposition with other disenfranchised groups. Minority groups often participate in each other's exploitation, as well as passively support control by the few. (Deegan, 1985, p. 52)

This draws attention to the important point that struggles within the ideological terrain generated by oppression do not occur just between the oppressors and the oppressed, but also amongst the oppressed themselves. A recent example of this is the way some feminists, in the analysis of the effects of community care policies on women, have portrayed disabled people as 'chronically dependent disabled' (Dalley, 1988). But it is not just the language in which the discourse is conducted which furthers the oppression of disabled people, but also their recipes for action, as in the case of the assertion that residential care is less oppressive to women than community care, therefore we need more residential establishments (Finch, 1984), ignoring the evidence that residential care is oppressive to disabled people (Miller and Gwynne, 1971; UPIAS, 1981).

To sum up, the process of identity formation in respect of disabled people cannot be understood without reference to the historical process leading to the formation of cultural images of disabled people. These cultural images have portrayed disabled people as less than or more than human and have been reinforced by professional conceptions of disability as adjustment to tragedy or the management of stigma. Such conceptions not only fail to take account of history and culture, but also locate the problem within the individual, failing to take account of the ways in which other factors like race or gender may structure the process of identity formation.

Thus the disabled identity is not formed simply through internal psychological processes but may be externally imposed. The implications of this are that this process is not fixed but can be changed by challenging dominant cultural images and by resisting the ideologies underpinning racism and sexism, for

> Whilst it is important to escape from an externally imposed handicapped identity, it is also important to resist the definitions of normality embedded in the ideologies of the able-bodied. (Leonard, 1984, pp. 197–8)

This resistance implies confronting disablism not just in the ideologies of the able-bodied but in the institutionalised practices stemming from these ideologies. This issue will be returned to in the final chapter, but before then consideration needs to be given to the ways in which disability has been constructed as a social problem and the policy implications of this construction, because these factors too can play an important part in the process of disabled identity formation.

6

The Social Construction of the
Disability Problem

So far, it has been suggested that the ideological construction of
disability has been determined by the core ideology of capitalism,
namely individualism; and that peripheral ideologies associated
with medicalisation and underpinned by personal tragedy theory
have presented a particular view of the disabled individual. But that
is only part of the story, for the category disability has also been
constructed as a particular kind of social problem. Hence

> We contend that disability definitions are not rationally deter-
> mined but socially constructed. Despite the objective reality, what
> becomes a disability is determined by the social meanings indi-
> viduals attach to particular physical and mental impairments.
> Certain disabilities become defined as social problems through
> the successful efforts of powerful groups to market their own self
> interests. Consequently the so-called 'objective' criteria of disability
> reflects the biases, self-interests, and moral evaluations of those in
> a position to influence policy. (Albrecht and Levy, 1981, p. 14)

SOCIAL POLICY AND DISABILITY

This process of social construction is not dependent solely on
individual meanings or the activities of powerful groups and vested
interests, for the category disability is itself produced in part by
policy responses to it. Thus, to take an extreme position,

> Fundamentally, disability is defined by public policy. In other
> words, disability is whatever policy says it is. This observation
> embodies an authoritative recognition that a disability implies a

78

problem or a disadvantage that requires compensatory or ame-
liorative action. The concept does not seek to specify whether the
problem is located in the individual or in the environment. Nor
does it attempt to identify the rationale for measures that are
taken in reaction to the perceived disadvantage. Nonetheless,
such policies represent an official belief that a disability consti-
tutes a disadvantageous circumstance that obliges a public or a
private agency to offer some type of response. (Hahn, 1985,
p. 294)

While not denying that policy definitions play an important role
in the social construction of disability, it is clear that these definitions are themselves socially constructed. And further, core and
peripheral ideologies have influenced this social construction to the
point where disability has become a problem of individual disadvantage to be remedied through the development of appropriate social
policies (Oliver, 1986; Borsay, 1986b).

Social policy analysis has been slow to recognise the role of
ideology in the development of social policies (George and Wilding,
1976) although in recent years it has been given a much more
central focus, (e.g. Wilding, 1982; Manning, 1985). However,
disability policy has not been subjected to any rigorous analysis of
its ideological underpinnings in the same way that many other social
problems have been deconstructed and even reconstructed.

Although little conscious attention has been devoted to the
problem, the recognition that public policy contains some unspoken assumptions about the level of physical or other abilities
required to sustain a person's life seems almost inescapable.
(Hahn, 1985, p. 296)

There are a number of reasons why these unspoken assumptions
or ideologies have not received much attention. Historically, disability policies have not developed in their own right and so

What is coming to be called disability policy is in fact an
aggregate of a variety of policies, each with quite different origins
and purposes, reflecting a historical situation in which concern for
disability has been intertwined with efforts to establish policy in
much broader issue areas. (Erlanger and Roth, 1985, p. 320)

These other policy areas have historically included issues of poverty, compensation for industrial workers and military personnel as well as broader issues of social control. Current broader issues include those of basic rights, the restructuring of social security programs and broader issues of health and welfare which are likely to impinge on the lives of disabled people among a variety of other groups. Thus it is not surprising that

> Rarely has public policy toward disability been introduced or analysed as 'disability policy'. Rather, it has been most often seen as a subset of some other, more general policy area such as labor, veterans, or welfare policy. (Erlanger and Roth, 1985, p. 320)

But this is no longer true in many capitalist countries which have begun to develop policies specifically in respect of disabled people. In Britain, for example, the Chronically Sick and Disabled Person's Act (1970) and the Disabled Person's (Services, Consultation and Representation) Act (1986), along with the appointment of a Minister for the Disabled in the 1970s, indicate moves towards the consideration of disability as a discrete policy issue, rather than as a mere adjunct to other policy issues.

Hence the explanation for the current failure to examine the hidden assumptions or ideologies underpinning these specific policy initiatives must lie elsewhere. Part of the answer is undoubtedly that these ideologies are so deeply embedded in social consciousness generally that they become 'facts'; they are naturalised. Thus everyone knows that disability is a personal tragedy for individuals so 'afflicted'; hence ideology becomes common sense. And this common sense is reinforced both by 'aesthetic' and 'existential' anxiety:

> widespread aversion toward disabled individuals may be the product of both an 'aesthetic' anxiety, which narcissistically rejects marked deviations from 'normal' physical appearances, and of an 'existential' anxiety, which may find an implicit or projected danger of dehabilitating disability even more terrifying than the inevitability of death. (Hahn, 1986, p. 125)

These anxieties have further contributed to the exclusion of disabled people from the mainstream of social and economic life and influenced policies that have placed disabled people in segregated establishments such as residential homes, special schools and day centres. And where policies have changed toward keeping people in the community, the ideology of personal tragedy theory has ensured that policies have been geared towards doing things to and on behalf of disabled people, rather than enabling them to do things for themselves.

However, according to Gramsci (1971) 'ideas are material forces', and as these material forces change, so will ideology. Thus, as capitalist economies have experienced a variety of fiscal crises, so the ideology underpinning welfare provision for disabled people has changed as well. No longer does it reflect tragedy and anxiety and the influence of benevolent humanitarianism. Rather, it reflects the burden that non-productive disabled people are assumed to be and the influence of monetarist realism. The ideological climate in which this finds expression focuses upon the notion of dependency.

Thus, the idea of dependency has been used to socially construct, or perhaps, more accurately, socially reconstruct the problem of disability, along with a whole range of other social problems which have been reconstructed in similar ways in many capitalist countries. John Moore, Minister for Health and Social Services in Britain, provided a reinterpretation of the development of the welfare state:

> For more than a quarter of a century after the last war public opinion in Britain, encouraged by politicians, travelled down the aberrant path toward ever more dependence on an ever more powerful state. Under the guise of compassion people were encouraged to see themselves as 'victims of circumstance', mere putty in the grip of giant forces beyond their control. Rather than being seen as individuals, people were categorised into groups and given labels that enshrined their dependent status: 'unemployed', 'single parent', 'handicapped'.
>
> Thus their confidence and will to help themselves was subtly undermined, and they were taught to think only Government action could affect their lives.
>
> This kind of climate can in time corrupt the human spirit. Everyone knows the sullen apathy of dependence and can compare it with the sheer delight of personal achievement. To deliberately set up a system which creates the former instead of

the latter is to act directly against the best interests and indeed the welfare of individuals and society. (Moore, 1988)

This reconstruction has been very successful at both the ideological and political level, giving rise to popular fears about the 'culture of dependency' and facilitating a restructuring of the welfare state. However, this account goes beyond the social constructionist explanation which tends to see ideas in general, and the idea of dependency in particular, as free-floating and natural. Rather, it argues that dependency is created through the application of particular social policies. Moore is not the first to point to the way in which social problems are created, particularly in respect of old people (Townsend, 1981; Walker, 1980), though there are disagreements about the mechanisms whereby this dependency is created. However, both views recognise that dependency is not constructed through changing ideas; it is created by a range of economic, political, social, technological and ideological forces. It is important at this point to distinguish between a social constructionist and a social creationist view of disability, as these distinctions have been noted elsewhere (Hahn, 1986; Oliver, 1985; Stone, 1985), but rarely discussed in any detail (Oliver, 1988).

The social constructionist world-view has been applied to a number of issues not unrelated to disability, including medicine (Freidson, 1970) and special educational needs (Barton and Tomlinson, 1981). This approach has thrown off the shackles of individualism and focused upon the cultural and social production of knowledge, showing that illness and special educational needs are not simply issues of individual pathology. But such an approach has been criticised for its influence on medical sociology (Bury, 1986) and on special education (Oliver, 1988), on the grounds of its difficulties in dealing with the problem of relativism and its tendency to reduce the historical process to that of label-changing.

The essential difference between a social constructionist and a social creationist view of disability centres on where the 'problem' is actually located. Both views have begun to move away from the core ideology of individualism. The social constructionist view sees the problem as being located within the minds of able-bodied people, whether individually (prejudice) or collectively, through the manifestation of hostile social attitudes and the enactment of social policies based upon a tragic view of disability. The social creationist

view, however, sees the problem as located
ised practices of society.

This leads to the notion of institutiona
has been developed in recent years to e
tion and anti-sexist and anti-racist pol
women and black people has persist
persisted because the implementation or .
awareness training) has focused on negative inu.
attitudes rather than on the behaviour of powerful organisa.
institutions. Hence 'although the battle for formal equality has bee.
relatively successful, the structures of disadvantage remain intact'.
(Gregory, 1987, p. 5)

The idea of institutionalised discrimination against disabled
people has also been used in recent years (Oliver, 1985; 1988) to
argue for anti-discrimination legislation in respect of disability, in
order to change behaviour rather than attitudes. Thus sexism,
racism and disablism are real and are socially created by a racist,
sexist and disablist society. The important advance that the social
creationist approach makes over the social constructionist one,
therefore, is that it does not assume that the institutionalised
practices of society are nothing more nor less than the sum total of
individual and collective views of the people who comprise that
society. To make the point again; ideas are not free-floating, they are
themselves material forces. The point, however, is not to choose
between these two views but to find a way of integrating them; a
start towards which has already been made.

Hence, studies founded on a socio-political orientation reflect a
significant attempt to bridge the gap between disability as a social
construct, or the relatively abstract concepts guiding research and
disability as a social creation, or the actual experience of disabled
citizens, which has been conspicuously absent in most previous
investigations of the issue. (Hahn, 1986, p. 132)

THE IDEA OF DEPENDENCY

Before considering the ways in which dependency is created, it is
necessary to define what is meant by the term. In common sense
usage, dependency implies the inability to do things for oneself and
consequently the reliance upon others to carry out some or all of the

everyday life. Conversely, independence suggests that the ...dual needs no assistance whatever from anyone else and this ...icely with the current political rhetoric which stresses competi- ...e individualism. In reality, of course, no one in a modern ...ndustrial society is completely independent: we live in a state of mutual interdependence. The dependence of disabled people there- fore, is not a feature which marks them out as different in kind from the rest of the population but different in degree.

There is obviously a link between this common sense usage of the term dependency and the way it is used in discussions of social policy, but these more technical discussions see at least two dimen- sions to the term. The first of these concerns the ways in which welfare states have created whole groups or classes of people who become dependent upon the state for education, health care, finan- cial support and indeed, any other provision the state is prepared to offer (Moore, 1988). The second focuses on the inability of indi- viduals or groups to provide their own self-care because of their functional limitations or impairments (Illsley, 1981). Both of these dimensions of dependency have figured large in current attempts to restructure welfare states by reducing the size and scope of state benefits and services and by shifting existing provision away from institutions and into the community.

These two dimensions have facilitated the development of reduc- tionist explanations of the phenomenon of dependency. Psycho- logical reductionism has focused upon the way the self-reliance of individuals and families has been eroded by the 'nanny state' and has thereby created 'pathological individuals'. Sociological reduc- tionism has focused upon the common characteristics of different groups, of which dependency is a major feature, thereby creating 'pathological groups'. Social science has often been actively involved in the creation of these reductionist explanations to the point where social scientists have been criticised for

> treating the concept of dependency as non-problematic. What is measured and how it is interpreted and used will depend to a large extent on the underlying theoretical and conceptual models adopted. These in turn reflect particular values and ideologies. (Wilkin, 1987, p. 867)

In recent years both sociological (Illsley, 1981) and feminist critiques of welfare provision (Finch, 1984; Dalley, 1988) have come to prominence, and while both have addressed the issue of dependency amongst disabled people, unfortunately they have done it in an uncritical way. Both have taken dependency as given; the former then seeking to identify the common characteristics of dependency groups and to explain, in sociological terms, the rising tide of dependents in the late twentieth century. The latter have sought to identify the physical and emotional costs of caring for dependents and to provide alternative approaches to the problem. Neither have sought to examine the concept of dependence critically and to suggest that the dichotomy dependence/independence is a false one; nor have they drawn on the growing body of work by disabled people themselves which has sought to suggest that disability, and hence dependency, is not an intrinsic feature of their impairments but is socially created by a disabling and disablist society. It is to some of the ways in which this dependency is created by the institutionalised practices of modern society, that the rest of this chapter will now turn.

AN ECONOMIC BASIS FOR THE CREATION OF DEPENDENCY

Work is central to industrial societies not simply because it produces the goods to sustain life but also because it creates particular forms of social relations. Thus anyone unable to work, for whatever reason, is likely to experience difficulties both in acquiring the necessities to sustain life physically, and also in establishing a set of satisfactory social relationships. Disabled people have not always been excluded from working but the arrival of industrial society has created particular problems, which have already been discussed in Chapter 2; disabled people often being excluded from the work process, because of the changes in methods of working and the new industrial discipline continuing to make meaningful participation in work difficult, if not impossible.

The onset of industrial society did not simply change ways of working, but also had a profound effect on social relations with the creation of the industrial proletariat and the gradual erosion of existing communities, as labour moved to the new towns. Industrialisation had profound consequences for disabled people therefore, both in that they were less able to participate in the work process and also because many previously acceptable social roles, such as begging or 'village idiot' were disappearing.

The new mechanism for controlling economically unproductive people was the workhouse or the asylum, and over the years a whole range of specialised institutions grew up to contain this group. These establishments were undoubtedly successful in controlling individuals who would not or could not work. They also performed a particular ideological function, standing as visible monuments to the fate of others who might no longer choose to subjugate themselves to the disciplinary requirements of the new work system. There were problems too in that it was soon recognised that these institutions not only created dependency in individuals but also created dependent groups. This led to fears about the 'burdens of pauperism' in the early twentieth century and the establishment of the Poor Law Commission. Similar concerns are around today, although, of course, the language is different, and current moves towards community care have a strong economic rationality underpinning them.

The reason for going over this again here is that the issues are still the same; disabled people are likely to face exclusion from the workforce because of their perceived inabilities, and hence dependency is still being created. And even where attempts are made to influence the work system, they do not have the desired effect because, on the whole, these programmes tend to focus on labour supply. Their aim is to make individual disabled people suitable for work but, while they may succeed in individual cases, such programmes may also have the opposite effect. By packaging and selling them as a special case, the idea that there is something different about disabled workers is reinforced and may be exclusionary rather then inclusionary. But it doesn't have to be this way, for

> The alternative, or more properly the supplement, to these programs is a focus on the demand side of the market, making people more employable and more a part of general social life by changing the social organisation of work and of other aspects of everyday life, through the removal of architectural barriers, nondiscrimination and affirmative action programs, mainstreaming in the schools, and so on. Until recently, there has been almost no concern with these possibilities. (Erlanger and Roth, 1985, p. 339)

It could, of course, be argued that government policy aimed at providing aids to employment and the adaptation of workplaces is precisely this approach, but it is nothing of the kind. These initiatives are all geared towards the supply side of labour, at making individual disabled people more economically productive and hence more acceptable to employers. There are no government incentives to create barrier-free work environments nor can Ford claim a grant if it wants to make its assembly line usable by all the potential workforce. Neither can other manufacturers wishing to design machinery or tools that are usable by everyone, regardless of their functional abilities, seek government assistance. There are virtually no attempts in modern capitalist societies that are targeted at the social organisation of work, at the demand side of labour. And given the size of the reserve pool of labour that currently exists in most capitalist societies, it is unlikely that such targeting will occur in the foreseeable future.

Given this historical and current situation it is hardly surprising that uncritical sociological reductionism can characterise disabled people and other groups as follows:

Their condition or situation makes them economically unproductive and hence economically and socially dependent. (Illsley, 1981, p. 328)

This is only partly true, however, for despite the high rates of unemployment in the industrialised world, the majority of disabled people of working age do have a job, and hence are economically productive. In addition, day centres, adult training centres and sheltered workshops make a considerable economic contribution by carrying out jobs that cannot easily be mechanised at wage rates that make Third World workers look expensive. But more importantly, this takes a narrow view of the economy and fails to recognise the importance of consumption. At present the benefits paid to disabled people amount to almost seven billion pounds a year (Disability Alliance, 1987) most of which 'will almost invariably be spent to the full' (George and Wilding, 1984). The numbers of firms now producing aids and equipment for disabled people and the seriousness with which motor manufacturers now take disabled motorists are testament to the important and 'productive' role that disabled people play in the economy of late capitalism; that is, an economy driven by consumption.

Following Illsley's narrow definition, the British royal family can be characterised as economically unproductive and economically and socially dependent. However, it is recognised that the institution of the monarchy performs an important economic role and they are not labelled 'dependents', except by their fiercest critics. That disabled people can be so labelled therefore, is due to a variety of other factors and is not solely a function of inaccurate assumptions about their role in the economy. Some of these other factors will now be considered.

A POLITICAL BASIS FOR THE CREATION OF DEPENDENCY

Policies enacted through the legislative process also have the effect of creating dependency and the current restructuring of the British welfare state is legitimated by the desire to reduce our 'culture of dependency'. In the case of disability, both the National Assistance Act (1948) and the Chronically Sick and Disabled Person's Act (1970) aimed to provide services for disabled people and in so doing reinforced

> the notion that people who happen to have disabilities are people who are 'helpless', unable to choose for themselves the aids to opportunity they need. (Shearer, 1981, p. 82)

More recently, the Disabled Person's (Services, Consultation and Representation) Act (1986), born out of both a recognition of the inadequacies of previous legislation as well as a wish to involve disabled people more in shaping their own destinies, is underpinned by the desire to improve the services for this 'dependent group'. It offers disabled people the right to be assessed, consulted and represented. However, it is noticeably silent on how these rights can be achieved in the face of recalcitrant local authorities, just as previous legislation was silent on how services could be obtained. In fact, this Act is yet a further extension of the professional and administrative approaches to the problems of disability, rather than an acknowledgement of disability as a human rights issue.

Yet in the late stages of the Second World War, the Disabled Person's (Employment) Act (1944) recognised that disabled people had a right to work. This legislation was not uninfluenced by the shortage of labour at the time or the collective guilt of seeing ex-servicemen, disabled while fighting for their country; but economic and social climates change, and these rights have never been enforced. Unsuccessful attempts to acknowledge the human rights issue involved, through the passage of anti-discrimination legislation, have surfaced in recent years but Parliament in its wisdom has never allowed the issue to receive legislative acknowledgement (Oliver, 1985). Thus the legislative framework remains locked into a professional and administrative approach to service provision. The ways in which service provision further perpetuates dependency will be considered in the next section, but first, one further political basis for the creation of dependency needs to be considered.

A further way in which dependency is, at least, reinforced is through the manner in which the discourse with regard to disability and social policy is conducted. From the patronising way politicians discuss disability in Parliament, through the failure of social policy analysts to examine critically the concept of disability (Oliver, 1986), to the failure of policymakers to consult with disabled people, this dependency is reinforced. Nor indeed when attention is turned to community care does the discourse alter, for community care implies 'looking after people' (Audit Commission, 1986). The nature of this discourse has recently been criticised thus:

> the need to be 'looked after' may well adequately describe the way potentially physically disabled candidates for 'community care' are perceived by people who are not disabled. This viewpoint has a long history, and a correspondingly successful application in practice – which has led to large numbers of us becoming passive recipients of a wide range of professional and other interventions. But, however good passivity and the creation of dependency may be for the careers of service providers, it is bad news for disabled people and the public purse. (BCODP, 1987, 3.2)

The political sphere thus plays a significant role in the social creation of dependency amongst disabled people in terms of both its legislative enactments and the way it conducts its discourse about policy. Further, it lays the foundations for the ideological climate within which services are provided and professional practice carried out.

A PROFESSIONAL BASIS FOR THE CREATION OF DEPENDENCY

There are a number of ways in which dependency is created through the delivery of professionalised services. The kinds of services that are available, notably residential and day care facilities with their institutionalised regimes, their failure to involve disabled people meaningfully in the running of such facilities, the transportation of users in specialised transport and the rigidity of the routine activities which take place therein, all serve to institutionalise disabled people and create dependency. While in recent years some attempts have been made to address this problem of dependency creation in these facilities, it remains unfortunately true that power and control continue to remain with professional staff. Many community services are delivered in similar ways and reinforce dependency; disabled people are offered little choice about aids and equipment; times at which professionals can attend to help with matters like toileting, dressing or preparing a meal are restricted; and the limited range of tasks that professionals can perform are limited because of professionalist boundaries, employer requirements or trade union practices.

The professional-client relationship can itself also be dependency-creating and the very language used suggests that power is unequally distributed within this relationship. Even when new professional approaches have been developed, as with the move from a medical to an educational approach to mental handicap, the problem remains for both approaches that they

> create a professional/client relationship which enshrines the professional in a world of exclusive and privileged knowledge, and consequently entombs the individual with learning difficulties in a fundamentally dependent role. (Brechin and Swain, 1988, p. 218)

Recent attempts to address this problem through changing the terminology from 'client' to 'user' or 'consumer' acknowledge that the problem exists, but do little to change the structures within which these power relations are located. Economic structures determine the roles of professionals as gatekeepers of scarce resources, legal structures determine their controlling functions as administrators of services, career structures determine their decisions about whose side they are actually on and cognitive structures determine their practice with individual disabled people who need help – otherwise, why would they be employed to help them? This is not just another attack on overburdened professionals, for they are as much trapped in dependency-creating relationships as are their clients. However, all is not as it seems, for in a fundamental sense it is professionals who are dependent upon disabled people. They are dependent on them for their jobs, their salaries, their subsidised transport, their quality of life and so on.

Thus if disabled people and professionals are trapped in these dependency-creating relationships, is there a way out of the trap? A false start has already been made through the promotion of the goal of independence which figures largely in the interventions of most professionals and the articulated aims of most disabled people. It has been a false start, however, because in advancing the idea of independence, professionals and disabled people have not been talking about the same thing. Professionals tend to define independence in terms of self-care activities such as washing, dressing, toileting, cooking and eating without assistance. Disabled people, however, define independence differently, seeing it as the ability to be in control of and make decisions about one's life, rather than doing things alone or without help. Hence it is 'a mind process not contingent upon a normal body' (Huemann, 1983).

If disabled people and professionals are ever going to engage in dependency-reducing rather than dependency-creating relationships, then the following advice from a disabled sociologist must be taken into account:

We must expand the notion of independence from physical achievements to sociopsychologic decision-making. Independent living must include not only the quality of physical tasks we can do but the quality of life we can lead. Our notion of human integrity must take into account the notion of taking risks. Rehabilitation personnel must change the model of service from doing something to someone to planning and creating services with someone. In short, we must free ourselves from some of the culture-bound and time-limited standards and philosophy that currently exist. (Zola, 1982, p. 396)

There are, of course, many other ways in which dependency is created, whether these are patronising social attitudes or the in-accessibility of the built environment, which constantly force disabled people to seek help. There is no need to consider these further here, but, we need now to consider the disabled individual who stands at the end of these economic, political and professional processes which create dependency, for both the experience of disability and of dependency are structured by these wider forces.

THE CREATION OF THE DEPENDENT INDIVIDUAL

A recent study of a small group of young disabled people attending a further education college found that

> Many of the students arrive in college with very negative self-image and poor self-esteem. Often they appear to have been conditioned into accepting a devalued social role as sick, pitiful, a burden of charity. (Hutchinson and Tennyson, 1986, p. 33)

Precisely how and why these disabled young people came to see themselves in this way now needs to be addressed.

All of the young people studied came to the college from special schools and there is no doubt that the medical hegemony in special education has hardly been challenged by recent legislative changes (Warnock, 1978; Education Act 1981). In practice medical need still predominates over educational need; disabled children still have operations (necessary and unnecessary) at times which fit in with the schedules of surgeons and hospitals rather than educational programmes, children are still taken out from classes for doctor's appointments or physiotherapy and the school nurse is still a more influential figure than the teachers (Bart, 1984). If children are brought up to believe, through experiencing a range of medical and paramedical interventions, that they are ill, we cannot be surprised if they passively accept the sick role.

But it is not only the intrusion of medicine into education which creates dependency through an acceptance of the sick role. They also see themselves as pitiful because they are socialised into accepting disability as a tragedy personal to them. This occurs because teachers, like other professionals, also hold to this view of disability, curriculum materials portray disabled people (if they appear at all) as pathetic victims or arch-villains and their education takes place in a context in which any understanding of the history and politics of disability is absent. The situation has been summarised as follows;

> The special education system, then, is one of the main channels for disseminating the predominant able-bodied/minded perception of the world and ensuring that disabled school leavers are socially immature and isolated. This isolation results in passive acceptance of social discrimination, lack of skills in facing the tasks of adulthood and ignorance about the main social issues of our time. All this reinforces the 'eternal children' myth and ensures at the same time disabled school leavers lack the skills for overcoming the myth. (BCODP, 1986, p. 6)

However, it is not just the educational environment which creates this dependency; the social environment plays a significant role in shaping the view that some disabled people hold of themselves as burdens of charity. To begin with, many of the traditional voluntary organisations for disabled people are quite shameless in the way they reinforce this charitable image through their fund-raising campaigns. Brandon (1988) accuses many of these organisations of 'rattling collection boxes on the most grossly disablist of themes'. The prime objective is to maximise income, regardless of the image presented. The unfortunate thing about this is that many of these organisations are not even aware of the way in which this approach creates dependency, and even if they are, then an instrumental, 'ends justifies means' philosophy is still often used (Hadley, 1988).

But it is not only voluntary organisations who beg on behalf of disabled people: some professionals are even employed by government agencies to do so. For example, disablement resettlement officers (DROs) employed by the Manpower Services Commission, instead of ensuring that employers are carrying out their legal duties under the Disabled Person's (Employment) Act, are given the task of persuading employers to give jobs to disabled people. Perhaps it is a mark of our civilisation in the industrialised world that we employ some people to beg on behalf of others; in many so-called less civilised societies, disabled people are at least accorded the dignity of begging on their own behalf.

Finally, many disabled people are forced into the position of passive recipients of the unwanted gifts or inappropriate services for to refuse such 'generosity' would confirm the 'fact' that disabled people have not come to terms with their disability and have a 'chip on their shoulder'. Examples of unwanted or unsuitable gifts are the wheelchairs designed by Lord Snowdon which turned out to be unusable by anyone who is paralysed; and examples of inappropriate services are the special vehicles, usually with the name of the donor written large all over the side, which are often used to transport disabled people. These are particularly used to carry disabled people to and from segregated facilities such as special schools, day centres and residential homes.

This chapter has suggested that social policies in respect of disability have been influenced, albeit unknowingly, by the core ideology of individualism. However, recently peripheral ideologies have shifted away from the ideologies of disability as personal tragedy and towards disability as dependency. This dependency is created amongst disabled people, not because of the effects of the functional limitations on their capacities for self-care, but because their lives are shaped by a variety of economic, political and social forces which produce it. Dependency is not a problem simply for the dependent individual but also for politicians, planners and professionals who have to manage (control) this dependency in accord with current social values and economic circumstance.

This problem and the political responses to it, both on the part of the state and of disabled people themselves, will be the subject of the next two chapters; for it is only through a proper consideration of the politics of disability that disabled people can be seen as not simply constituted by the variety of structural forces already considered in this book, but also as active agents in the process of constituting society in its totality.

7
The Politics of Disablement – Existing Possibilities

The final two chapters will consist of an analysis of the current provision of services, a consideration of future trends within the capitalist state and a more speculative and visionary discussion of alternative possibilities. A critique of the current restructuring of the welfare state along lines set by the political right will be provided and this will be followed by a consideration of alternative conceptualisations provided by the political left. Finally it will be argued that we need to move beyond the traditional left–right framework for understanding political activities, with its associated and traditional notions of interest representation, and move towards an understanding of the disability movement as part of the development of new social movements, characteristic of late capitalism. Only then will we begin to grasp the importance of the politics of disablement.

THE RESTRUCTURING OF THE WELFARE STATE – THE ELIMINATION OF DEPENDENCY?

Since the mid-1970s there has been a world economic recession, one result of which has been to call into question both the nature and future of welfare states in the industrial world. This questioning has usually been raised within the language of crisis, of which there are at least three dimensions;

(a) a crisis in the welfare state in that it was not meeting social needs,

(b) a crisis of the welfare state in that it was creating needs that it could not meet,

(c)   a crisis by the welfare state in that the rising cost of welfare was
creating a crisis of capitalism itself.

Further,

> The crisis definition is now being used as an ideological basis for
> reducing social expenditure, changing redistributive patterns in
> disfavour of the marginal groups and reducing government res-
> ponsibility in social policy. (Oyen, 1986, p. 6)

While both the precise nature of this crisis and the ideological
response to it differ from industrial country to industrial country, all
have had broadly similar experiences. In Britain, the left have
broadly subscribed to the view that there is a crisis in the welfare
state and that the solution is to increase public expenditure on it.
The right, on the other hand, have subscribed to the view that there
is a crisis of the welfare state and, if not properly managed and
controlled, it could indeed become a crisis of the capitalist state. As
the right have held political power for most of this period, it is their
view of the nature of the crisis which has shaped the process of
restructuring the welfare state. A major underpinning of the ideological basis for this restructuring has been the issue of dependency.
Reductions in expenditure, changes in redistribution and the
gradual withdrawal of the state from people's lives, have all been
legitimated on the grounds of the need to reduce dependency.
There is little doubt, with regard to disabled people, that their
experiences of the welfare state coincide with both the 'crisis in' and
'crisis of' dimensions. In other words, they have not received all the
services they need and in many cases those services that they have
received have created or reinforced their dependency. So, it has to be
said that future policy options stemming from either (or both) of
these dimensions are unlikely to succeed in reducing dependency,
whether it be physical or social. Simply increasing public expenditure will only serve to lock disabled people further into the
dependency-creating relationships already described, and reductions and redistributions will condemn disabled people to isolation
and loneliness in the community or institutionalisation in residential
care.
In the previous chapter, primacy was given to the economic basis
for creating dependency, but it has to be concluded that in the

current political climate, there is little scope for intervening in the economy, for

> Social policy has been assigned ... to the role of intervening in a natural order of economic relationships to modify their outcome in the interests of 'social' goals. In both capitalist and state socialist societies, social policy has operated as a 'handmaiden' to the economy. (Walker, 1984, p. 33)

Hence the chances of tackling this economic basis for the creation of dependency amongst disabled people 'are slim because the same societal forces which manufacture disability also mitigate against a structural response' (Borsay, 1986a, p. 188).

This does not imply the complete pessimism of an economically determinist position which is an accusation sometimes made of sociology in general, and Marxist sociology in particular. While the economic may be determining 'in the last instance', there is considerable scope within what Gramsci called the state (conceptualised as a social relation) and civil society for individuals, groups, interests or classes to act autonomously. The point being made here is not that economics determines politics, but the more limited one that the politics of social policy is circumscribed by economic considerations.

Certainly, in the current political climate, the Conservative Government in Britain shows little inclination to intervene in the economy, and as far as social policy and state welfare is concerned, it is actively withdrawing through the strategy of privatisation (Le Grand and Robinson, 1984). This privatisation has three aspects; reductions in state provision, reductions in state subsidies and reductions in state regulation; and is underpinned by the rhetoric of targeting, consumer choice and dependency reduction. It is emphasised by recent government reports (DHSS, 1988; NISW, 1988) which stress the need to give consumers (a key word in the new rhetoric) more choice of, and control over, services. In reality, no one, except those on the extreme right, see all welfare services being provided by the private market as the main objective, but rather it is the reductions in the role of the state within a 'mixed economy of welfare' which is the main goal.

As far as disabled people are concerned, this privatisation is not something that has occurred only in recent years. Services such as

residential care and special education have been provided by
organisations like the Cheshire Foundation and the Spastics Society
almost since the inception of the welfare state, and all the evidence
suggests that these services create dependency in exactly the same
way as state services. More recently the privatisation of some cash
payments for some severely disabled people who would previously
have had statutory rights to such payments, through the establishment of a trust fund to be administered by the Disablement Income
Group, is only likely to reinforce dependency by furthering the
image of disabled people as burdens of charity.

It is, perhaps, ironic that the model for providing these privatised
services is that of the supermarket; the argument being that
packages of care can be purchased just as customers purchase
products from supermarket shelves. Ironic, because many disabled
people find shopping in supermarkets difficult if not impossible
because of physical access, difficulties in reaching shelves and the
fact that products and packaging are tailored to the needs of the
modern nuclear family and not to the needs of individuals. In short,
supermarkets offer a limited range of products which suit the needs
of particular groups in society and if not in these groups, then the
consumer is not sovereign, as the rhetoric would have it. Thus, for
many disabled people, the supermarket model of provision is
unlikely to offer anything substantially different from the provision
of state services; that is to say, little choice over what is provided and
little control over how it is provided. Further, the supermarket
model, utilising the rhetoric of consumerism has been criticised, for

> In sum ... this model is a 'harmless version' of consumerism – it
> requires little serious change, but much public visibility. It is
> about the appearance, not substance, of change. (Winkler, 1987,
> p. 1)

What the supermarket is alleged to offer, but clearly does not, is
choice and control. The key issue for the future as far as the left is
concerned is whether the 'crisis in' the welfare state can be resolved
by offering users of services choice and control. The traditional view
from the left suggests that it can, by the modification and adaptation
of first principles:

> The challenge that faces us is not the choice between universalist

and selective services. The real challenge resides in the question: what particular infrastructure of universalist services is needed in order to provide a framework of values and opportunity bases within and around which can be developed acceptable selective services provided as social rights, on criteria of needs of specific categories, groups and territorial areas and not dependent upon individual tests of means? (Titmuss, 1968, p. 122)

To update the language somewhat, it should be possible to allow for choice and control in service provision within a universalist infrastructure if consumers have social rights to these services and if there are mechanisms whereby the needs of groups and communities, whether local or interest communities, can be articulated by them, themselves. This view is therefore articulated by some of the new thinkers on the left where it is only the words, not the ideas, that have changed.

The goal would be truly universal services; that is, for the community and not separate client groups, distributed according to need rather than ability to pay. They would be based on small local areas, as far as possible, to enable democratic involvement and control. This would help to counteract paternalism and dependence. (Walker, 1984, p. 43)

Specifically, as far as disabled people are concerned, the left in Britain, in the shape of the Labour Party (Meacher *et al.*, 1986), has attempted to switch the emphasis away from needs and on to rights. But it has become clear that if disabled people are to have social rights to services, then the legislative framework must do more than simply list these services (Chronically Sick and Disabled Person's Act) or provide professional and administrative approaches to their provision (Disabled Person's [Services, Consultation and Representation] Act). This inevitably implies the necessity for anti-discrimination legislation which would not only provide public affirmation of the unacceptability of discrimination against disabled people, but also, if properly drafted, a framework for the enforcement of service delivery and a mechanism for professional accountability. In both political and policy-making terms, an emphasis on social rights rather than individual needs, suggests a move away from the ideology of individualism and the beginnings of attempts to address the creation of dependency at both political and professional levels.

By itself it would not be enough, of course, as the experience in the areas of race and gender demonstrate (Gregory, 1987). Therefore an essential adjunct would be legislation facilitating complete freedom of information which goes beyond current attempts to provide access to information held on computers and in local authority files. The locked medical cabinets would need to be opened and the unofficial documents that are kept as ways of avoiding information-disclosure (as with current practices which require information to be provided to parents under the statementing regulations of the Education Act [1981]), would need to be made available.

Finally, a mechanism whereby the needs of groups and communities can be articulated, needs to be developed. This can only be accomplished through the adequate funding and resourcing of organisations controlled and run by disabled people which have been going from strength to strength throughout the world in the 1980s. Significantly, there is some evidence that these organisations of disabled people find it easier to flourish in the underdeveloped rather than the industrial world. This is due, in part, to the resistance to change of bureaucratic and professional structures in the industrial world, but also to the existence of a large and powerful sector of traditional organisations for the disabled who remain locked into dependency-creating service provision and attitudes, and who, consequently, have vested interests in maintaining the *status quo*.

None of these developments by themselves, or an incremental approach to them, is likely to prove successful. Anti-discrimination legislation without freedom of information and a supportive network of disabled people, will simply mean that the lawyers will get rich; freedom of information by itself will mean that individual disabled people will be subjected to professional mystification and slight of hand; and support for the disabled people's movement without a framework which guarantees basic human rights will leave the movement politically emasculated. But an integrated programme as suggested above, could provide a means of addressing the problems of dependency-creation at both political and professional levels, and hence go some way to resolving the 'crises' both, in and of, the welfare state, at least as far as disabled people are concerned.

Given that this integrated programme could represent a way

forward in terms of offering a more appropriate basis for the provision of welfare state services for and with disabled people, the crucial question then concerns the possibilities of getting this and/or other programmes on to the political agenda. There are two ways in which this question can be examined; firstly, in terms of direct participation through the ballot box, and secondly, through pressure-group activity. It is these political strategies that now need to be considered.

THE POLITICAL PARTICIPATION OF DISABLED PEOPLE

That disabled people constitute a potentially powerful political force there can be no doubt, for according to Fry (1987) a recent MORI poll in Britain found that 9% of the public (18+) considered themselves to be disabled and 27% said that another member of their family was disabled. This study (Fry, 1987) looked at the political participation of disabled people in the General Election of 1987, and found that many disabled people did not even appear on the electoral register; others, particularly blind and deaf people, were denied access to all the information necessary to make an informed choice; and other disabled people, postal and proxy voting notwithstanding, found the problem of transport and physical access to polling stations too daunting to allow them to exercise their right to vote.

There are two further ways in which it is difficult for disabled people to participate within the party system. Firstly, many local constituency headquarters are inaccessible and hence it is very difficult for them to become grassroots activists and to feed in disability issues at this level. Secondly, although there are examples of disabled politicians at the local and national level, it is also very difficult for many disabled political activists to offer themselves as candidates at local or national elections, for the problems of both campaigning and door-to-door canvassing may prove to be impossible.

Even if these barriers to political participation were removed, it would not necessarily mean that the disabled population would cohere into an active political force to which all political parties would need to take notice. There are a number of reasons for this.

To begin with there is a great deal of variety within the disabled population as a whole – differences in social class, age, sex, family circumstances and clinical conditions – as well as the fact that disability may have developed after political commitments had been established. In addition, many disabled people do not necessarily regard themselves as disabled, or even if they do, would not contemplate joining an organisation for disabled people. Finally, as a consequence of disability, some people may disengage from political activity, either because their physical impairment poses limitations of a physical or psychological kind, or because they are aware that in many contexts they lack any basis for exercising power, e.g. through the withdrawal of their labour. (Oliver, 1984, p. 23)

Extending this analysis, it has been suggested also that the medical approach to disability has fostered artificial divisions within the disabled population (Borsay, 1986a).

But these divisions do not arise simply from the medical approach, for the state also provides services in such a way as to foster divisions within the disabled population. Hence, it gives tax allowances to blind people but not to other categories of disability, mobility allowances to those who cannot walk but not for those who can, and higher pensions and benefits for those injured at work or in the services than for those with congenital disabilities or those who have had accidents. This is not an unintentional consequence of state provision but a deliberate tactic which the state has developed in its dealings with other groups and can summed up as 'divide and rule'.

This idea of disabled people as a group divided amongst itself has obvious implications for any notions of class-based political activity:

The myriad of disability-specific programs and policies, the segregation of disabled people, the inability to gain access to organised society, to experience an integrated and adequate education, to obtain meaningful employment, and to socially interact and participate has resulted in a politically powerless and diffuse class of people who are unable to coalesce with other groups of disabled people on common issues, to vote, to be seen or heard. This class has accepted the stigma and caste of second-hand citizenship and the incorrect judgement of social inferiority. (Funk, 1987, p. 24)

This description of the political situation fits in neatly with the 'underclass thesis' developed to explain the political situation of black people.

The usefulness of this idea of an underclass is still being debated within sociology, centring around the issue of whether an underclass is a sub-group of the working class or a group relegated to the margins of society on the basis of personal or group characteristics. In either case disabled people as an underclass are likely to remain powerless and marginalised, at least as far as organised political activity is concerned.

Thus it is unlikely that disabled people can expect the party political process to serve their interests well. If we return to the issue of anti-discrimination legislation, while it is true that this issue has been forced on to party-political agendas, and indeed, several bills have even been introduced in Parliament, nonetheless, all of these have been defeated, usually covertly, but on one occasion, overtly through the operation of the party political system; that is, through a sustained campaign by Conservative whips to ensure that their party members voted it down (Oliver, 1985). Hence, disabled people can hardly expect to articulate and achieve their political ends through the party system, and this raises the question of whether they can expect pressure-group activity to serve them better.

THE POLITICS OF PRESSURE-GROUP ACTIVITY

From the mid-1960s onwards, it became clear that, despite rising affluence, a number of groups were not sharing in the new material and social benefits that were being created, and that traditional political activity was not even getting these issues on to the political agenda. This resulted in the creation of new kinds of pressure groups who were likely to campaign around single issues of one kind or another. Groups like Shelter and the Child Poverty Action Group are examples of these, and specifically, in the area of disability, the Disablement Income Group is the most prominent example. The establishment of these groups

was a reaction to what was perceived to be the fraudulent character of British democracy. There were of course special conditions which explained the new expression of protest. Public expectations had been running high. The policies of successive Governments had been built on relatively full employment and steadily increasing national wealth. This meant that the views and interests of workers, pensioners and others were believed to weigh more heavily than they had done before the war in the conduct of national affairs . . . Some groups – like the elderly, one-parent families and sick and disabled people – were observed to have been left behind in the race for prosperity. (Townsend, 1986, pp.i–ii)

If, then, disabled people could not get issues on to the political agenda through the normal processes of political participation, then this raises the issue of whether the avenue of pressure-group activity was likely to be more successful. The most sophisticated analysis of this so far is provided by Borsay (1986a) who draws heavily on the framework provided by Cawson (1982). Cawson suggests that pluralist analyses of pressure-group politics are now inadequate because of the nature of the 'corporate state', and that it is necessary to distinguish between competitive groups, whose members share a common interest, and corporate groups, whose members share a common position within the division of labour. Needless to say, it is the latter who have most influence on the political decision-making process. As most disability organisations are of the former kind, their partnership with government (Oliver, 1984) is unlikely to have much influence.

This partnership does not inevitably banish the needs and opinions of physically disabled people from sight, but the allegiance of corporate professional interests to economic development stacks the cards against their faithful representation in the shaping and administration of policy. (Borsay, 1986a, p. 15)

It is not, however, simply a matter of the structural location of these disability organisations that leads to such pessimism. As most of these organisations are registered as charities, direct and overt political activity is precluded. But more importantly, these disability organisations have, over the years, built up a relationship with the state, or the 'establishment' as Borsay calls it, which gives them credibility, but little power.

The string of more formal voluntary organisations or charities, which for many years have doubled up as pressure groups in the field of physical handicap, meet the same structural barriers to change, but the status which flows from their long traditions and their connections with the 'establishment' give them a credibility and aura in government circles which more recent (and perhaps more radical) groups of disabled people cannot easily imitate. (Borsay, 1986a, p. 16)

This credibility has been based upon history and tradition rather than the claim to representativeness of these organisations, whose 'key decision-makers' are usually salaried professional staff who articulate their own assumptions about the needs of disabled people rather than the needs of disabled people as they themselves express them. Two recent examples of this are the attempts of the Government with the public support of RADAR to abolish the Quota, established under the Disabled Person's (Employment) Act, 1944, and the opposition of the Spastics Society to anti-discrimination legislation. Pressure from individual disabled people and from organisations controlled and run by disabled people forced public about-turns in both cases.

There is one further aspect of the politics of disability as pressure-group activity that needs to be considered; that of minority-group politics. In the wake of the Civil Rights and Women's Movements in the United States in the 1960s, it was suggested that disabled people should seek to articulate and claim their rights to full citizenship on the basis of their own particular needs as a minority group (Hahn, 1986). However, there are problems with this approach, for

The minority group approach basically argues that disabled people should be brought into the American political system as another interest group. The structure of decision making isn't attacked. Instead the idea is to improve the odds that the disabled will be recognized as having legitimate demands. (Liggett, 1988, p. 271)

Using what she calls 'an interpretive approach', based on the work of Foucault, Liggett takes her criticisms further than this. Just as earlier, it was argued that professional interventions in the lives of disabled people were structured by certain discursive practices, so, she argues, is the politics of disability. Thus the minority group approach

> is double-edged because it means enlarging the discursive practices which participate in the constitution of disability. In other words, the price of becoming politically active on their own behalf is accepting the consequences of defining disability within new perspectives, which have their own priorities and needs. The new perspectives then become involved in disciplining disability. (Liggett, 1988, p. 271)

Thus, accepting disabled people as a minority group also involves the accepting of the disabled/non-disabled distinction; accepting the 'normalising' society.

This has implications for disabled people seeking to gain control over their own lives, for

> in order to participate in their own management disabled people have to participate as disabled. Even among the politically active, the price of being heard is understanding that it is the disabled who are speaking. (Liggett, 1988, p. 273)

While not disagreeing with this analysis of the politics of disability as minority group activity, Liggett's problems arise when she suggests alternative political strategies. These strategies involve 'reflection' and sometimes the acceptance, sometimes the rejection of disabled identities, depending upon the specifics of particular situations.

However, such strategies would inevitably look like special pleading and further, move away from the strategies disabled people have chosen for themselves; that is, the personal and public affirmation of disabled identities and the demands that disabled people be accepted by and integrated into society as they are; that is, as disabled people.

Thus, the structural position of these organisations, their relationship to the state, their non-representativeness in terms of the needs and wishes of disabled people and their acceptance of the normalising of society, lead to the inevitable conclusion that

> for disabled people ... the chances of immediate and radical reform of social policies are slim. (Borsay, 1986a, p. 19)

It is hard to disagree with this conclusion when analysing disability pressure-group activity from a pluralist, corporatist or minority group position, but an analysis based upon the idea of 'new social movements' within late capitalism, can lead to very different conclusions. However, that is the subject of the next chapter and no discussion of pressure-group activity would be complete without some discussion of the single, most sustained example of pressure-group activity within the field of disability in Britain; the campaign for a national disability income.

A NATIONAL DISABILITY INCOME

The campaign for a national disability income began in 1965 with the formation of the Disablement Income Group by two disabled housewives. This group provided a major focus for pressure-group activity and published plans for a national disability income comprising two elements; a disablement costs allowance and an income maintenance scheme. A decade later, the Disability Alliance was formed, initially comprising over fifty voluntary organisations, which has now grown to over ninety, and they put forward their own proposals which were broadly similar to those of DIG. Recently both have updated their plans (DIG, 1987; Disability Alliance, 1987), which are, again broadly similar, except that the Alliance proposals plan to incorporate a separate, independent benefit for those who care for a disabled person, whereas DIG argue that if disabled people were given a proper, adequate income, it would be unnecessary to pay carers separately.

There are difficulties in assessing the success or failure of these pressure-group activities over the last twenty years, though it has to be said that a national disability income has not yet become a reality. On the other hand, all of the major political parties have made public commitments to the establishment of such a scheme (Disability Alliance, 1987, pp. 4–5), but have couched these pronouncements with get-out clauses such as 'when economic circumstances permit' and 'as a matter of priority'.

Despite these expressed commitments, no substantial progress has been made towards the introduction of a comprehensive disability income scheme. The past decade has instead seen a series of piecemeal changes which, although sometimes useful, have failed to correct the longstanding anomalies in social security provision for people with disabilities. Furthermore, in a number of vital areas, benefits have been cut and new anomalies created. (Disability Alliance, 1987, p. 5)

So, during the past twenty years, there have been some incremental improvements, usually connected to the performance of the economy, but there have also been reversals.

There are a number of reasons why this sustained campaign has been unsuccessful. To begin with, both DIG and the Alliance have suffered from the problem already referred to, that as registered charities, they have been unable to campaign in an overt political way. They have therefore found it necessary to divide their organisations into two component parts in order to retain their charitable status and to continue with political activities. In addition, both organisations have found it necessary to set up information and advisory services in order to steer disabled people through the maze of benefits and to help individuals to receive all the benefits they are entitled to. Finally, they have carried out research to demonstrate that the financial position of disabled people is considerably worse than that of their able-bodied counterparts. Hence, neither organisation has been able to concentrate solely on pressure-group activities.

Both groups can also be criticised for taking a somewhat naïve view of the political process in that their campaigning is based upon three assumptions; that evidence must be produced to show the chronic financial circumstances of disabled people; that proposals for a national disability income must be properly costed to show that the burden on the economy will be marginal; and that sustained pressure must be mounted to hammer these points home to the political decision-makers. This approach has been called 'the social administration approach' and has been criticised for its assumptions about consensual values, rational decision-making, its unproblematic view of the state and its failure to acknowledge, let alone consider the role of ideology. Perhaps the only thing that can be said in its favour is that

If the empiricist study of consensual solutions to defined social problems did not exist, it would be necessary to invent it:

democratic welfare capitalism presupposes the social administration approach. (Taylor-Gooby and Dale, 1981, p. 15)

What the income approach to disability fails to understand, therefore, is that political decisions are not made on the strength of particular cases, but in ways whereby the capitalist system itself benefits, regardless of the appearance of consensual values concerning the need for a national disability income. The establishment of such a scheme implies the paying of one group of people a sufficient income for not working to enable them to have a quality of life comparable to another group of people who do work. This, of course, has enormous implications for any system which requires its members to produce sufficient goods and services to sustain the material life of the population, and indeed for its ideological underpinnings which emphasises the value of those who do work and denigrates those who do not. In short, the fundamental question of whether a national disability income is achievable within capitalism, has never been addressed.

This failure to address fundamental issues has brought criticism of both DIG and the Disability Alliance from the more 'populist' organisation, the Union of the Physically Impaired Against Segregation (UPIAS). The two major criticisms of this approach are that it concentrates on a symptom (i.e. the poverty of disabled people) rather than the cause (i.e. the oppression of disabled people by society), and that both organisations have moved away from representing disabled people and instead present an 'expert' view of the problem. The logical conclusion to this approach, according to this analysis, is to make things worse, because such an approach would be 'expert-led' in that it would require detailed individual assessments. The consequence of this for disabled people would be that

We would be required to sit alone under observation on one side of the table, while facing us on the other side, social administrators would sit together in panels. We would be passive, nervous, deferential, careful not to upset the panel: in short, showing all the psychological attributes commonly associated with disability. It would be the social administrators who would gain strength, support and confidence from colleagues on the panel. A token number of the more privileged physically impaired people might be included, as they are in the Alliance. But the whole approach would reinforce the historical and traditional situation whereby physically impaired people are made dependent upon the thinking and decisions of others. (UPIAS, 1976, p. 18)

This debate about 'expert' or 'mass' representation in respect of pressure group activity has continued into the 1980s, with Townsend (1986) claiming that these groups can only be 'representative' in certain senses.

But what they can do is commit themselves unreservedly to the interests of millions of poor people, call representative injustices to public notice and exchange blow with blow in an expert struggle with the Government over the effects, implications and constitutional niceties of policy. (Townsend, 1986, p. v)

But like UPIAS before it, BCODP denies the claims of such groups to be representative in any sense, suggests that expert representation can only be counter-productive, and argues that the only way forward is to fully involve disabled people in their own political movement.

If this analysis is correct, then it is, perhaps, fortunate that a national disability income is likely to be unachievable within capitalist society. However, it does raise the cash-versus-services debate in respect of provision for disabled people. Both left and right agree that the key issue is to give disabled people choice in respect of services and control over their own lives. In theory, this can then be polarised into a market solution by giving people sufficient cash (i.e. a national disability income) to purchase their own services, or a state solution by making services and professionals accountable (i.e. anti-discrimination legislation, freedom of information and a strong disability movement). In practice, these solutions are not mutually exclusive and neither DIG or the Alliance would argue that service developments were unnecessary, nor would UPIAS argue against an adequate income for disabled people if it were part of a wider package of reforms.

The crucial issue from a political point of view, however, is whether the traditional, single-issue pressure-group campaign for a national disability income is any longer a relevant tactic for the post-capitalist world to which we are moving. The following chapter will suggest that the politics of disablement can only be properly understood as part of the new social movements which are part of post-capitalist society.

8
The Politics of Disablement – New Social Movements

The preceding analysis has suggested that disabled people cannot look to either the welfare state or traditional political activities to effect considerable material and social improvements in the quality of their lives. The only hope, therefore, is that the disability movement will continue to grow in strength and consequently have a substantial impact on the politics of welfare provision. This chapter will thus consider the emergence of new political activities, which have been characterised as 'new social movements', and discuss the emergent disability movement as part of this new phenomenon. The structure and tactics of the disability movement will be considered, along with the role of the state, before, finally, an assessment of future possibilities will be made.

THE EMERGENCE OF NEW SOCIAL MOVEMENTS

Just as earlier social theorists had been concerned to understand the far-reaching changes that were occurring as a result of industrialisation; so after a period of relative stability, from the 1960s onwards academics have once again begun to address this issue of social change (Kumar, 1978). Changes in the economy from one driven by consumption rather than production, the rise in technology, changing occupational patterns, social disorganisation affecting family and social life, increasing crime and hooliganism, crises in the welfare state, the ecological crisis and various kinds of political unrest have all been features of capitalism in the late twentieth century. This has led some sociologists to characterise the end of the twentieth century as the era of late capitalism or to herald the coming of post-industrial or post-capitalist society.

This has had an influence on the political system and since the 1970s there has been the emergence of many new movements comprising of neighbourhood groups, environmentalists, the unemployed, welfare recipients, minority groups and 'the generally disenfranchised' (Castells, 1978; Touraine, 1981; Boggs, 1986). These movements have been seen as constituting the social basis for new forms of transformative political action or change. These social movements are 'new' in the sense that they are not grounded in traditional forms of political participation through the party system or single-issue pressure-group activity targeted at political decision-makers.

Instead, they are culturally innovative in that they are part of the underlying struggles for genuine participatory democracy, social equality and justice, which have arisen out of 'the crisis in industrial culture' (Touraine, 1981). These new social movements are consciously engaged in critical evaluation of capitalist society and in the creation of alternative models of social organisation at local, national and international levels, as well as trying to reconstruct the world ideologically and to create alternative forms of service provision. It is in this sense that Touraine (1981) defines such movements as 'socially conflictful' and 'culturally oriented forms of behaviour'.

Before considering the relationship between the disability movement and these new social movements, it is necessary to consider the history of the disability movement in Britain itself. Crucial to this consideration is the distinction between organisations for the disabled and organisations of disabled people. In practice, this centres on the issue of who controls and runs the organisation, and in reality, organisations of disabled people are those organisations where at least 50 per cent of the management committee or controlling body must, themselves, be disabled. These organisations have emerged in the last twenty years, but this emergence must be placed in the context of the growth of the traditional voluntary organisation for the disabled.

THE HISTORY OF THE DISABILITY MOVEMENT

The rise of traditional voluntary organisations can be linked to the rise of capitalism itself and by the middle of the nineteenth century there were a considerable number of small societies for the blind in existence. This led to the establishment of the Royal National Institute for the Blind (RNIB) in 1868, and throughout the latter half of the century similar organisations grew up for the welfare of the deaf and the crippled. The growth in these organisations signified a move away from 'individual concern for the handicapped' to a concern to promote the welfare of particular groups (Topliss, 1979), and such groups were successful in raising public awareness and encouraging the state to take on particular responsibilities.

This trend continued into the twentieth century and it was not until the establishment of the welfare state, with its principle of cradle-to-grave security, after the Second World War, that further changes occurred. Effectively this meant that the state took over complete responsibility for welfare provision for disabled people, though in practice, the state was happy to allow voluntary organisations to continue to provide services, sometimes in partnership and sometimes as sole providers. Ultimately, however, responsibility now lay with the state. There was some concern, at the time, that this might adversely affect these voluntary organisations, but, in practice, the state was never able to assume total responsibility, and voluntary organisations continued to grow at local and national levels, often with state support.

Despite the affluence of the postwar years, coupled with legislative changes and increases in service provision, it soon became clear that disabled people, among other groups, were not having all their needs met and, often, even those needs that were acknowledged, were being met in inappropriate or oppressive ways. The traditional voluntary organisations, locked into a partnership approach with the state, were unable to do anything about this, and disillusion set in, leading to the formation of single-issue groups like DIG. Further, as has already been discussed, this disillusion soon spread to the new single-issue pressure groups, and more and more disabled people came to realise that, if they were going to improve the quality of their own lives, they had to do it themselves, prompting the rise of self-help and populist forms of organisation (Oliver, 1984).

Such groups would not have emerged had the existing voluntary organisations been adequately articulating and representing the needs and wishes of disabled people. Hence, these newly-emerging groups were critical of the traditional groups on a number of grounds. A major thrust of this criticism of organisations run by non-disabled people is that they operate within a framework which assumes that disabled people cannot take control of their own lives and, therefore, require the 'charitable' assistance of well-meaning professionals, voluntary workers or politicians (Battye, 1966; Crine, 1982; BCODP, 1988).

Closely allied to this criticism is the view that people who run organisations for rather than of disabled people operate within a medical rather than a social model of disability which locates the problems faced by disabled people within the individual rather than being contingent upon social organisation (Oliver, 1983). Finally, these groups are criticised on the grounds of the interests they actually serve, whether they be of the establishment, the careers of the professional staff or the personal aggrandisement of key individuals through the honours system. According to one commentator, these key individuals

> can get sucked into the old boy network, even if they are women, (and few of the big-timers are) and rapidly get out of touch, for example, with life inside the run-down council estates and the mental handicap hospitals. As they get more powerful, they get more out of touch. Life looks different from the inside of a BMW. (Brandon, 1988, p. 27)

There were also a number of external influences on the disability movement, noticeably the similar rise of movements of black people and women, and the passage of anti-discrimination legislation in these areas. Similarly, in some other countries, such legislation had been passed in respect of disabled people, but in Britain, at least, the Government set its face against such an approach (Oliver, 1985). There are two other events which gave further impetus to the disability movement, and helped to give it a sense of cohesiveness at national and international levels.

The first of these was the United Nations plan to designate 1981 International Year for the Disabled. Its very title reinforced the idea that disabled people should have things done for them and it was only after considerable lobbying that the initiative became the International Year of Disabled People. That did not stop many of the planned events from reinforcing the charitable images of disabled people, but disabled people set themselves the task of exploiting the opportunity IYDP offered them and formed their own national, umbrella organisation, the British Council of Organisations of Disabled People, which has gone from strength to strength since then, and now claims a membership of nearly 50 independent organisations representing over 100 000 disabled people nationally.

The second event was the plan of Rehabilitation International (an organisation for the disabled) to publish its own Charter on Disability, the central aim of which was

> To take all necessary steps to ensure the fullest possible integra-
> tion of an equal participation by disabled people in all aspects of
> the life of their communities.

At the very same conference where this Charter was being discussed, the organisation turned down a proposal from a group of disabled people that Rehabilitation International should, itself, become an organisation of disabled people, by making sure that it was controlled by disabled people themselves. So, while integration and participation could be recommended to everyone else, it was not for Rehabilitation International itself. Perhaps it was fortunate that the organisation took this blinkered view, for the decision led directly to the formation of Disabled Peoples' International (DPI), the international equivalent of BCODP.

One final point needs to be made in respect of the history of the disability movement in Britain, and that concerns the coming to power of the Thatcher Government in 1979. This Government was committed to reducing public expenditure, minimising the role of the state and privatising a whole range of services. Throughout the eighties, this has had profound implications for disabled people; inadequate existing services have become even more inadequate, specific political goals like a national disability income and antidiscrimination legislation are further away than ever, and some rights and benefits have been removed altogether. The traditional disability organisations have been able to do little about this, and this has reinforced the message to the disability movement that the only thing it can do is to 'organise' (Ryan, 1988). Hence for the first time, in 1988 disabled people in this country organised their own opposition to the Social Security Act (1986) and took to the streets in London and other big cities as a way of registering their protests.

This brief history of the rise of disability organisations can be summarised in the following way.

A TYPOLOGY OF DISABILITY ORGANISATIONS

Earlier (Oliver, 1984), a typology of disability organisations was constructed to describe their range and scope and to provide a key to their historical development. With some amendments and additions, the following is intended to provide a profile of such organisations and their historical development.

1 Partnership/patronage

Organisations for disabled people; charitable bodies; provision of services (often in conjunction with statutory agencies); consultative and advisory role for professional agencies; Examples: RADAR, RNIB, Spastics Society, Joint Committee on Mobility.

2 Economic/parliamentarian

Primarily organisations for disabled people; single issue; parliamentary lobbying and research (mainly on economic issues); legalistic bodies; may or may not be party political. Examples: DIG, Disability Alliance (part of the 'poverty lobby' associated with Child Poverty Action Group, Fabian Society, etc.).

3 Consumerist/self-help

Organisations of disabled people; self-help projects and other activities aimed at problem-solving and providing services to meet self-defined needs of members; may or may not be political/campaigning groups also; may work in collaboration with local or national statutory and/or voluntary agencies. Examples: Spinal Injuries Association, Derbyshire Centre for Integrated Living.

4 Populist/activist

Organisations of disabled people; political activist groups; often antagonistic to the partnership approach; primary activities focused on 'empowerment', personal and/or political; collective action and consciousness raising. Examples: UPIAS, Sisters against Disablement, British Deaf Association.

5   *Umbrella/co-ordinating*

Organisations of disabled people; collective groupings of organisations comprising consumerist and/or populist groups; rejecting of
divisions within the disabled population based upon clinical condition, functional limitation or age; may function at local, national or
international levels; primarily political organisations aiming to
facilitate the empowerment of disabled people by a variety of means.
Examples: Greenwich Association of Disabled People, BCODP, DPI.

There are a number of points that need to be made about this
typology. First, it is intended to be flexible and descriptive and will
not necessarily fit all organisations conveniently within it. Secondly,
it does provide a trajectory of historical development, with organisation 1 being the earliest and organisation 5 being the newest on the
scene. Finally, and most importantly, in referring to the disability
movement as a new social movement, only organisations 3–5 are
contained within this definition. It is to the claim that these
organisations can be called a new social movement that attention
now needs to be given.

THE DISABILITY MOVEMENT AS A NEW SOCIAL MOVEMENT

There are four characteristics of new social movements that can be
considered as relevant to the disability movement as a new social
movement. The first of these is that they tend to be located at the
periphery of the traditional political system and in fact, sometimes
they are deliberately marginalised (Hardin, 1982). This is certainly
true of the disability movement, which does not have the same
relationship to the state as do the organisations for the disabled,
either in terms of consultation procedures, lobbying or, indeed,
resourcing. For example, RADAR, the umbrella 'organisation for',
is usually given a grant of £225 000 per year by the DHSS, whereas
its 'organisation of' counterpart, BCODP is lucky to get £10 000 per
year.

However, this does not mean that the political significance and
meaning of the disability movement can be taken to be marginal and
neither can its transformative potential. New social movements in

general do have great significance and meaning in the changing political circumstances that are currently occurring.

The changing nature of political interests is most clearly focussed around what have come to be termed as 'new social movements'... The new social movements are characterised by not only a greater willingness to employ a wide variety of forms of political action, but also by an underlying orientation towards political values that have widespread ramifications. In particular their underlying scheme of values stress the importance of political participation and personal self-actualisation in ways that have implications for the forms that political behaviour takes. (Weale, 1988, pp. 1–2)

This definition accurately fits in with the emergence of self-help/consumerist groups within the disability movement, both in terms of the importance such groups place on personal self-actualisation, and their willingness to follow pro-active strategies towards what, ultimately, become political goals.

Self-help groups were slow to develop ... but they have flourished and have become a powerful source of mutual support, education and action among people affected by particular health concerns or disabilities ... while learning and working together, disabled people can combine their power to influence social and political decisions that affect their lives. (Crewe and Zola, 1983, pp. xiii–xiv)

However, the development of self-help strategies can initially be purely practical, rather than explicitly political. One case study highlights the way in which the self-help approach is often a response to the perceived failings in professional service provision. Thus while the initial impetus was to encourage disabled people 'to solve their problems themselves and not have them solved for them', there was also a further aim which was 'to identify the needs of the membership as a whole and articulate them, both to statutory agencies and political parties at both a local and a national level' (Oliver and Hasler, 1987, p. 116).
Hence,

The self-help movement is ... but one part of the struggle. It is a pre-requisite for change, but neither the sole nor the sufficient avenue. We must deal as much with social arrangements as with self-conceptions; one, in fact, reinforces the other. (Zola, 1979, p. 455)

This link between the personal and the political is often an integral feature of these new social movements:

To varying degrees and in varying ways the new movements also seek to connect the personal (or cultural) and political realms, or at least they raise psychological issues that were often submerged or ignored... (Boggs, 1986, p. 51)

A specific form of self-help, more or less unique to the disability movement and, perhaps, the clearest practical illustration of the ways in which the disability movement corresponds with general definitions of new movements, can be found in the increasing numbers of Centres for Independent and Integrated Living (CILs) being established both in the UK and in other countries, including the United States, Australia, Canada and Japan. CILs represent both an attempt to achieve self-actualisation, and a form of direct action aimed at creating new solutions to problems defined by disabled people themselves (Oliver, 1987b).

The second characteristic of new social movements is that they offer a critical evaluation of society ... as part of 'a conflict between a declining but still vigorous system of domination and newly emergent forms of opposition' (Boggs, 1986, p. 4). Ideologically, the Independent Living Movement which led to the establishment of the first CILs in California and other parts of the United States in the late 1960s, also represents an explicit critique of prevailing social structures and the position of disabled people within them. The rationale behind the Independent Living Movement was that the obstacles to self-actualisation were perceived to be the result of living in hostile physical and social environments and the fact that what services were provided, were restricting rather than enabling. The movement set about attempting to change this situation, firstly by redefining the problem in this way and then by setting up alternative kinds of service-provision under the control of disabled people themselves.

The situation in the United States, where CILs emerged, is

different from that in Britain in three important respects. Firstly, the US has a tradition of seeing some problems as human rights issues, both in terms of constitutional history and the influence of the civil rights movement. Secondly, there were very few statutory services available to disabled people in America and thirdly, there was no large, organised voluntary sector of organisations for the disabled. In Britain, there was no human rights tradition, though there were many state services and a large voluntary sector, both of which had proved to be inadequate. Hence, the tactics of CILs in Britain had to reflect this different context and the issue here was more concerned with controlling services than creating them. Thus the change of name from centres for independent to integrated living and the change in tactics also.

> CILs are poised at the fulcrum of the contemporary struggle to tilt the balance of history in favour of a fairer and more equitable future for disabled people. The Derbyshire Coalition argues that the key to social change is the active participation of people who are themselves disabled and that CILs ... can exert a beneficial influence on the existing service infrastructure in Britain. (Davis, 1983, p. 16)

More generally, this feature of the Independent Living Movement as a political strategy, prefigures the increasingly dominant view that disability is not merely socially constructed, but socially created as a form of institutionalised social oppression like institutionalised racism or sexism (Sutherland, 1981; Abberley, 1987). The Independent Living Movement by no means circumscribes the disability movement as a whole. It is, however, one of its principal dimensions, both as an underlying ideology and a practical political strategy. Furthermore, its development illustrates the influence on the disability movement of

> other contemporary movements, such as civil rights, consumerism, self-help, demedicalisation/self-care, deinstitutionalisation. The significance of independent living cannot be understood apart from the contributions of these other movements. (De Jong, 1983, p. 5)

The significance of these other social movements is that they are taken as evidence of the emergence of a 'post-materialist paradigm'. The common denominator amongst these movements, including the disability movement, is that they typically emerge as a response to the perceived failure of existing political institutions and strategies to achieve the objectives of a particular social group as they themselves define them. This has been particularly true in the United States where the civil rights tradition has profoundly influenced the disability movement.

> The civil rights movement has had an effect not only on the securing of certain rights but also on the manner in which these rights have been secured. When traditional legal channels have been exhausted, disabled people have learned to employ other techniques of social protest. (De Jong, 1983, p. 12)

Lacking such a tradition in Britain, and not even having basic rights enshrined in law through anti-discrimination legislation, the disability movement in this country has been more circumspect in terms of tactics, although the lessons of the American movement have been noted and there have been a few organised boycotts, sit-ins and street demonstrations.

The third characteristic of new social movements resulting from fundamental changes in the constitution of the political agenda has been

> an increasing predominance of ... 'post-materialist' or 'post-acquisitive' values over those that have to do with income, satisfaction of material needs and social security. (Offe, 1980, p. 12)

While it is certainly true that the disability movement is concerned with issues relating to the quality of life of disabled people, it is also true that many disabled people still face material deprivation as well as social disadvantage and the movement is centrally concerned with this. It would be inaccurate to attempt to characterise the disability movement as stemming from a middle-class and disabled elite concerned only with their own quality of life, as Williams (1983) attempts to do in his critique of the Independent Living Movement.

A final characteristic of new social movements is that they

sometimes tend to focus on issues that cross national boundaries, and hence they become internationalist. This is certainly true of the disability movement and at DPI's Second World Congress, the objectives and strategies underlying the international movement were clearly defined around the central issues of empowerment and of disabled people acting collectively to achieve collective goals. It was noted by the Congress that

> political action aimed at governmental bodies – or at private groups or individuals, was more likely to produce results than through a legislative or constitutional route. Countries which had passed legislation favourable to disabled people, did not necessarily find that improved conditions followed – or that disabled people had more control over their lives as a result. The prerequisite for successful action lay in the proper organisation of disabled persons' groups, and the development of a high level of public awareness of disability issues... This did not necessarily mean that disabled people's organisations were in an antagonistic relationship to established organisations which were not controlled by disabled people. But it did mean that our own organisations should assert that they were the true and valid voice of disabled people and our needs. (DPI, 1986, p. 21)

The discussion so far has indicated that the disability movement can be considered as part of new social movements generally. The crucial question this therefore raises, is what does it mean for political action in general and the possibility of improving the quality of life for disabled people in particular?

NEW DIRECTIONS FOR THE FUTURE

Thus far, attempts to consider the meaning and significance of these new social movements generally (Boggs, 1986; Laclau and Mouffe, 1985) have usually taken place within a framework derived from the work of Gramsci (1971). Within this framework there are three discrete areas that need to be considered; the economy, the state and civil society, all given a sense of unity by the concept of hegemony. For Gramsci, the economy referred to the dominant mode of production; the state consisted of all state-funded institutions in-

cluding the political, the bureaucratic and the means of violence; the
term civil society

> connotes the other organizations in a social formation which are
> neither part of the processes of material production in the
> economy, nor part of state funded organizations, but which are
> relatively long-lasting institutions supported and run by people
> outside of the other two major spheres. (Bocock, 1987, pp.33–4)

The importance of the concept of hegemony in Gramsci, was that
it claimed that dominance, or leadership of all the people, could
never be simply reduced to dominance in the economic sphere, but
could be established within the state or civil society. Thus, politics,
not economics, can have a central role in the establishment of
hegemony, and within Gramsci's framework, this politics can take
place both within the state and civil society, although

> The borderline between state and civil society is a constantly
> shifting one and one which has to be negotiated, maintained and
> continually re-adjusted over time. (Bocock, 1987, p. 34)

To put the matter simply, political activity within the state comprises traditional party politics and corporatist pressure group activities; political activity within civil society comprises the activities of
the new social movements. The crucial issue for these new social
movements thus becomes one of how far they can effect political and
social change, either by shifting power across the borderline and
away from state political institutions, or by exerting greater and
greater external influence on these existing institutions.

It is within this framework that consideration can be given to the
significance of the disability movement as a new social movement.
The role of the economy has already been considered and somewhat
pessimistic conclusions arrived at. However, there is one aspect of
economic development that needs to be considered at this point, and
that is the role and potential of new technology, before giving
consideration to the state, civil society and the possibilities of
developing counter-hegemonic political structures.

A major factor to be considered in the development of post-
capitalist society is the influence of new technological developments
on the economic, social and material needs of disabled people.

Finkelstein (1980), while not specifically calling Phase 3 of his model post-capitalism, is clear where both the problem and the solution lies.

> Disabled people, also, no less than able-bodied people, need to express their essential human nature by moulding the social and material environment and so influence the course of history. What stands in the way, (at a time when the material and technological basis for solving the human and material needs of disabled people have mostly been solved), is the dominance of phase 2 attitudes and relationships. Such attitudes take society and, indeed, the dependency relationship as given. (Finkelstein, 1980, p. 39)

But not all commentators see the issue as one of outdated attitudes, moulding technology in particular directions, but point to the fact that technology itself will not necessarily produce or equally distribute its benefits (Illich, 1973; Habermas, 1971). These techno-logical developments have not been universally welcomed in terms of health care in general (Reiser, 1978; Taylor, 1979) nor disability in particular (Oliver, 1978). Zola, writing from his own experience has suggested that

> Technology can do too much for those of us with disabilities. The machines that technology creates may achieve such completeness that they rob us of our integrity by making us feel useless. (Zola, 1982, p. 395)

And he applies this analysis not just to the development of machines, gadgets and prostheses, but also to what he calls 'the over-technicalization of care'.

> To be handled by a machine or animal, where once I was handled by a person, can only be invalidating of me as a person. (Zola, 1982, p. 396)

Further, in terms of its effects on the work system and the material and social environments, it may be oppressive rather than liberat-ing. In a review of changes in the work system in what he calls 'post-industrial society', Cornes (1988) discusses both the optimistic and pessimistic views of the effects of new technology on the work

opportunities of disabled people. He suggests that such developments can be viewed optimistically,

> New jobs and new opportunities to organise and locate work on
> an entirely different basis using new technologies are increasingly
> being perceived as offering even more grounds for optimism. This
> is because such new jobs, in which physical requirements are
> replaced by electronic skill, strength and precision are particularly
> suitable for people with disabilities, and because new develop-
> ments in communications have increased opportunities for home-
> based employment. (Cornes, 1988, p. 15)

But he then sounds a cautionary note, suggesting that many
disabled people may not have the educational opportunities or
training potential to take advantage of such opportunities. Further,
the new skills that will be required to master new technology may
require a degree of confidence and independent thinking that many
disabled people currently lack. Finally, he suggests that many
disabled people are already falling behind in the mastery of these
skills 'because of problems of access, mobility, finance and discrimi-
natory attitudes' (Cornes, 1988).

He agrees with Finkelstein's (1980) analysis, that the problem is
that while we are in phase 3 in terms of economic and technological
developments, we, nonetheless, remain locked into phase 2 attitudes, or in Cornes' terms, that 'existing policies, programmes,
attitudes and expectations may be too dependent on the institutional
arrangements, values and ideals of an industrial society' (Cornes,
1988). And he goes on to locate the solution as being in the hands of
the disability movement itself.

> Their successful participation in all spheres of life within post-
> industrial society – economic, cultural and political – will depend
> greatly on the extent to which they themselves and their suppor-
> ters can lay claim to and exercise that right not only during the
> transition from school to work but throughout their lifetimes.
> (Cornes, 1988, p. 17)

If then, the disability movement is central to ensuring that
technology is used to liberate rather than further oppress disabled
people, then a clear understanding of its double-edged nature needs

to be developed within the movement. A start in this direction has been made by recognising that the mentality which allows technology to be used for evil purposes is the very same mentality which facilitates the oppression (and indeed, even the creation) of disabled people.

> Relentlessly, the connection between disability and the bomb becomes clear. The mentality that made Cheshire a compliant participant in the mass creation of disability at Hiroshima is the same mentality which made him the instigator of the mass incarceration of disabled people in a chain of segregated institutions. In the first case he went over the tops of the heads of disabled people in a B29 bomber, in the second he went over our heads in the name of charity. Increasingly, over the years, both actions have come to attract our abhorrence ... we have to find the strength to INSIST that our representative organisations are fully involved in decisions about the dismantling of disabled apartheid. And we have to add our *instant* voice to the clamour for *world disarmament* – with the aim of removing for all time, this particular and horrifying cause of unnecessary disability. (Davis, 1986b., p. 3)

But, in order to challenge what might be called attitudes (Finkelstein, Cornes), mentality (Davis) or more properly, in the context of this analysis, ideology, then clearly the disability movement must work out an appropriate political strategy. As has already been indicated, this cannot be through traditional political participation in parties or pressure groups, but has to be addressed in terms of the relationship between the disability movement and the state, the second element within Gramsci's (1971) framework.

The relationships of these new social movements in general to the state have been considered in some detail and raise crucial issues of political strategy.

> If social movements carry forward a revolt of civil society against the state – and thus remain largely outside the bourgeois public sphere – they typically have failed to engage the state system as part of a larger democratizing project. In the absence of a coherent approach to the state, political strategy is rendered abstract and impotent. (Boggs, 1986, p. 56–7)

On the other hand, to engage in an uncritical relationship to the state, is to risk at best, incorporation and absorption, and at worst, isolation and marginalisation and perhaps, ultimately, oblivion.

Leaving aside the question of whether the state represents specific interests or is relatively autonomous, the disability movement has to decide how it wishes such a relationship to develop. Should it settle for incorporation into state activities with the prospect of piecemeal gains in social policy and legislation with the risks that representations to political institutions will be ignored or manipulated? Or, should it remain separate from the state and concentrate on consciousness-raising activities leading to long-term changes in policy and practice and the empowerment of disabled people, with the attendant risks that the movement may be marginalised or isolated?

In practice, it cannot be a matter of choosing one or the other of these positions, for the disability movement must develop a relationship with the state so that it can secure proper resources and play a role in changing social policy and professional practice. On the other hand, it must remain independent of the state to ensure that the changes that take place do not ultimately reflect the establishment view and reproduce paternalistic and dependency-creating services, but are based upon changing and dynamic conceptions of disability as articulated by disabled people themselves. Such is the nature of a crucial issue facing the disability movement over the next few years and the complexities of the task should not be underestimated.

In order, however, to develop an appropriate relationship with the state, all new social movements, including the disability movement, must establish a firm basis within civil society.

The important point is that these movements, as emergent, broad-based agencies of social change, are situated primarily within civil society rather than the conventional realm of pluralist democracy. Further, the tendency toward convergence of some movements (for example, feminism and the peace movement) gives them a radical potential far greater than the sum of particular groups. Even though their capacity to overthrow any power structure is still minimal, they have begun to introduce a new language of critical discourse that departs profoundly from the theory and practice of conventional politics. (Boggs, 1986, p. 22)

Thus, because these movements are developing within the separate sphere of civil society, they do not risk incorporation into the state, nor indeed, do they need to follow a political agenda or strategy set by the state. Hence, they can engage in consciousness-raising activities, demonstrations, sit-ins and other forms of political activity within civil society. Further, they can develop links with each other so that their potential as a whole is greater than that of their constituent parts. Finally, the relationship to organised labour needs to be renegotiated, which means that labour will have 'to confront its own legacy of racism, sexism and national chauvinism' because

> The complex relationship between labour and social movements, class and politics – not to mention the recomposition of the work force itself – invalidates any scheme that assigns to labour a hegemonic or privileged role in social transformation. (Boggs, 1986, p. 233)

As far as the disability movement is concerned, its growth and development have been within the realm of civil society. It has used consciousness and self-affirmation as a political tactic and has begun to be involved in political activities such as demonstrations and sit-ins outside the realm of state political activities. By reconceptualising disability as social restriction or oppression, it has opened up the possibilities of collaborating or cooperating with other socially restricted or oppressed groups.

But it has also crossed the borderline between the state and civil society by developing its own service provision, sometimes in conflict and sometimes in cooperation with state professionals, and has, on occasions, engaged in interest representation within the state political apparatus. The issue of crossing the borderline to the economy and establishing links with organised labour, however, has yet to be properly addressed. It could be said that as well as overcoming its racism, sexism and chauvinism, organised labour has to overcome its disablism too. While the labour movement has been broadly supportive in wishing to retain the Quota, established by the Disabled Person's (Employment) Act, 1944, it has been disablist in its resistance to changing work-practices to facilitate the employment of disabled people and to rewriting job specifications to enable disabled people to get the kind of personal support they need to live better lives in both the community and residential care.

COUNTER-HEGEMONIC POLITICS

The concept of hegemony is a unifying one in that it contextualises the relationships between the economy, the state and civil society. While hegemony may be exercised in all three realms,

> In any given historical situation, hegemony is only going to be found as the partial exercise of leadership of the dominant class, or alliance of class fractions, in some of these spheres but not in all of them equally successfully at all times. (Bocock, 1986, p. 94)

And this, of course, raises the possibility of counter-hegemonic tendencies emanating from civil society rather than from traditional political institutions or changes within the economy, for

> Contemporary social movements are thus hardly marginal expressions of protest but are situated within the unfolding contradictions of a rapidly changing industrial order, as part of the historic attempts to secure genuine democracy, social equality, and peaceful international relations against the imperatives of exploitation and domination. (Boggs, 1986, p. 3)

And it is not unrealistic to suggest that only when peace, democracy and equality have been secured, that the social restrictions and oppressions associated with disability can be eradicated. This chapter has suggested that the disability movement has a central role to play in the eradication of these restrictions and oppressions as part of the emergent new social movements.

It has to be admitted that nowhere in the world have these new movements been successful in overturning the *status quo*. Their significance has been in placing new issues on to the political agenda, in presenting old issues in new forms and indeed, in opening up new areas and arenas of political discourse. It is their counter-hegemonic potential, not their actual achievements, that are significant in late capitalism.

> To say that the new movements have a counter-hegemonic potential is also to suggest that they have emerged in opposition (at least partially) to those ideologies that legitimate the power structure; technological rationality, nationalism, competitive indi-

vidualism, and, of course, racism and sexism. (Boggs, 1986, p. 243)

Perhaps, after reading this book, disablism can be placed at the end of the above quote, for a central theme of it has been that disability merits sociological analysis and demystification in precisely the same way as all the other 'isms. Unfortunately, up to now

the sociology of disability is both theoretically backward and a hindrance rather than a help to disabled people. In particular, it has ignored the advances made in the last 15 years in the study of sexual and racial equality and reproduces in the study of disability parallel deficiencies to those found in what is now seen by many as racist and sexist sociology. (Abberley, 1987, pp. 5–6)

In eradicating the social restrictions and oppressions of disability, both the disability movement and non-disablist sociology have a part to play.

Postscript: The Wind is Blowing

There is a sense in which this book can be read both pessimistically and optimistically. The argument suggests that the dominant view of disability as an individual, basic, medical problem is created by the productive forces, material conditions and social relations of capitalism. The chances of transcending these forces, conditions and relations are therefore intrinsically bound up with the possibilities of capitalism itself being transcended. These possibilities do not appear to be likely to materialise in the foreseeable future, for, even allowing the idea of post-capitalist society, such a society appears more as an extension of capitalist forces, conditions and relations than as a transition on the road to socialism.

However, disability does not appear as an individual, tragic and medical problem in all societies that have existed historically nor in some that exist currently. So it may be that the material conditions and social relations of disability can be improved without waiting upon the possibility of the transcending of the productive forces of capitalism itself. Thus there are grounds for optimism from this more limited view.

The most important factor in this optimism is the rise of a strong, vibrant and international disability movement within a decade. But there are other grounds for optimism also. The sheer size of the disability problem (Martin *et al.*, 1988) with its associated appalling material conditions (Martin and White, 1988) will inevitably mean that some political action will be taken. The criticism of existing service provision that are emerging from even establishment organisations (Fiedler, 1988; Beardshaw, 1988) should ensure that changes take place therein. The contradictions that many professional groups, including the medical profession (Royal College of Physicians, 1986), are experiencing in relation to their obligations to

their employers and their duties to their clients, mean that professional practice is being re-evaluated. Finally, the appearance of
many more disabled people on the streets and in general social
intercourse is beginning to change public consciousness about
disability.

Marx himself knew that the course of general development was
influenced by 'accidents'. The 'accidents' referred to above have all
occurred at a particular historical point, making change inevitable.
The wind is indeed blowing; the direction that wind takes will
depend upon more than just disabled people themselves.

Bibliography

Aall-Jilek, L. (1965). 'Epilepsy in the Wapagoro Tribe', *Acta Psychiat. Scand*, 61, 57–86.

Abberley, P. (1987). 'The Concept of Oppression and the Development of a Social Theory of Disability' *Disability, Handicap and Society*, Vol. 2, no. 1, 5–19.

Abberley, P. (1988). 'The Body Silent: A Review', *Disability, Handicap and Society*, Vol. 13, no. 3.

Abbot, P., and Sapsford, R. (1987). *Community Care for Mentally Handicapped Children* (Milton Keynes: Open University Press).

Ablon, J. (1981). 'Stigmatized Health Considerations', *Social Science and Medicine*, Vol. 15B.

Abrams, P. (1982). *Historical Sociology* (London: Open Books).

Ainley, S., Becker, G., and Coleman, L. (1986). *The Dilemma of Difference: A Multidisciplinary View of Stigma* (London: Plenum Press).

Albrecht, G. (ed.) (1981). *Cross National Rehabilitation Policies: A Sociological Perspective* (London: Sage).

Albrecht, G., and Levy, J. (1981). 'Constructing Disabilities as Social Problems', in Albrecht (ed.).

Albrecht, G., and Levy, J. (1984). 'A Sociological Perspective of Physical Disability', in Ruffini (ed.).

Althusser, L. (1971). *Lenin and Philosophy and Other Essays* (London: New Left Books).

Anderson, E. (1979). *The Disabled Schoolchild* (London: Methuen).

Audit Commission (1986). 'Making a Reality of Community Care' (London: HMSO).

Baldwin, C., and Smith, R. (1984). 'An Evaluation of the Referral and Rehabilitation Process Among the Minority Handicapped', *International Journal of Rehabilitation Research*, Vol. 7, no. 3.

Barker, R., Wright, B., Meyerson, L., and Gonick, M. (1953). 'Adjustment to Physical Handicap and Illness' (New York: Social Science Research Council).

Barrett, D., and McCann, E. (1979). 'Discovered: Two Toed Man', *Sunday Times Colour Supplement*, n.d.

Bart, D. (1984). 'The Differential Diagnosis of Special Education's Managing Social Pathology as Individual Disability', in Barton and Tomlinson (eds).

Barton, L. (ed.) (1988). *The Politics of Special Needs* (Brighton: Falmer Press).

Barton, L., and Tomlinson, S. (eds) (1981). *Special Education: Policy, Practice and Social Issues* (London: Croom Helm).

Barton, L., and Tomlinson, S. (eds) (1984). *Special Education and Social Interests* (London: Croom Helm).

Battye, L. (1966). 'The Chatterley Syndrome' in Hunt, P. (ed.), *Stigma – The Experience of Disability* (London: Chapman).

BCODP (1986). 'Disabled Young People Living Independently', (London: British Council of Organisations of Disabled People).

BCODP (1987). 'Comment on the Report of the Audit Commission' (London: British Council of Organisations of Disabled People).

BCODP (1988). 'The British Council of Organisations of Disabled People' (unpublished Draft Policy Statement).

Beardshaw, V. (1988). 'Last on the List: Community Services for People with Physical Disabilities' (London: Kings Fund Institute).

Becker, G., and Arnold, R. (1986). 'Stigma as a Social and Cultural Construct', in Ainley *et al.*

Bennett, A. (ed.) (1978). *Recent Advances in Community Medicine* (London: Heinemann).

Blaxter, M. (1980). *The Meaning of Disability*, 2nd edn (London: Heinemann).

Bocock, R. (1987). *Hegemony* (London: Tavistock).

Boggs, C. (1986). *Social Movements and Political Power* (Philadelphia: Temple University Press).

Bonwich, E. (1985). 'Sex Role Attitudes and Role Reorganisation in Spinal Cord Injured Women' in Deegan and Brooks (1985).

Borsay, A. (1986a). *Disabled People in the Community* (London: Bedford Square Press).

Borsay, A. (1986b). 'Personal Trouble or Public Issue? Towards a Model of Policy for People with Physical and Mental Disabilities', *Disability, Handicap and Society*, Vol. 1, no 2.

Brandon, D. (1988). 'Snouts among the Troughs', *Social Work Today*, 10 November 1988.

Brechin, A., Liddiard, P., and Swain, J. (eds) (1981). *Handicap in a Social World* (London: Hodder & Stoughton).

Brechin, A., and Swain, J. (1988). 'Professional/Client Relations: Creating a "working alliance" with People with Learning Difficulties', *Disability, Handicap and Society*, Vol. 3, no. 3.

Brenton, M., and Jones, C. (ed.) (1985). *The Year Book of Social Policy in Britain 1984–5* (London: Routledge & Kegan Paul).

Brisenden, S. (1986). 'Independent Living and the Medical Model of Disability', *Disability, Handicap and Society*, Vol. 1, no. 2.

Brittan, A., and Maynard, M. (1984). *Sexism, Racism and Oppression* (Oxford: Blackwell).

Burton, M. (1983). 'Understanding Mental Health Services: Theory and Practice', *Critical Social Policy*, No. 7.

Bury, M. (1986). 'Social Constructionism and the Development of Medical Sociology', *Sociology of Health and Illness*, Vol. 8, no. 2.

Campling, J. (1981). *Images of Ourselves* (London: Routledge & Kegan Paul).

Castells, M. (1978). *City, Class and Power* (London: Macmillan).

Cawson, A. (1982). *Corporatism and Welfare: Social Welfare and State Intervention in Britain* (London: Heinemann).

Cohen, S. (1985). *The State and Social Control* (London: Polity Press).

Cole, S., and Miles, I. (1984). *Worlds Apart* (Brighton: Wheatsheaf).

Comte, A. (1855). *The Positive Philosophy* (New York: Calvin Blanchard).

Confederation of Indian Organisations (1987). 'Double Bind: To be Disabled and Asian' (London: Confederation of Indian Organisations).

Confederation of Indian Organisations (1988). 'Asians and Disabilities' (London: Confederation of Indian Organisations).

Connelly, N. (1988). 'Care in the Multi-racial Community' (London: PSI).

Conrad, P., and Schneider, J. (1980). *Deviance and Medicalisation: From Badness to Sickness* (St Louis: Mosby).

Cornes, P. (1988). 'The Role of Work in the Socialisation of Young People with Disabilities in a Post-Industrial Society', Paper presented at OECD Conference, 'Adult Status for Youth with Disabilities' (Sigtuna: Sweden).

Cottam, P., and Sutton, A. (eds) (1985). *Conductive Education: A System for Overcoming Motor Disorder* (London: Croom Helm).

Crewe, N., and Zola, I. (1983). *Independent Living for Physically Disabled People* (London: Jossey-Bass).

Crine, A. (1982). 'Was Ever a Battle Like This?', *Community Care*, 27 September 1982.

Dalley, G. (1988). *Ideologies of Caring: Rethinking Community and Collectivism* (London: Macmillan).

Davis, A. (1987). 'Women with Disabilities: Abortion or Liberation', *Disability, Handicap and Society*, Vol. 2, no. 3.

Davis, K. (1983). 'Consumer Participation in Service Design, Delivery and Control' (Clay Cross, Derbyshire: Coalition of Disabled People).

Davis, K. (1986a). 'Developing Our Own Definitions – Draft for Discussion' (London: British Council of Organisations of Disabled People).

Davis, K. (1986b). 'DISABILITY and the BOMB – The Connection' (Clay Cross, Derbyshire: Coalition of Disabled People Newsletter).

Deegan, M. (1985). 'Multiple Minority Groups: A Case Study of Physically Disabled Women' in Deegan and Brooks (eds).

Deegan, M., and Brooks, N. (ed.) (1985). *Women and Disability: The Double Handicap* (New Brunswick: Transaction Books).

De Jong, G. (1983). 'Defining and Implementing the Independent Living Concept' in Crewe and Zola (eds).

DHSS (1988). 'Community Care: Agenda for Action' (London: HMSO).

Disablement Income Group (DIG) (1987). 'DIG's National Disability Income' (London: DIG).

Disability Alliance (1987). 'Poverty and Disability: Breaking the Link' (London: Disability Alliance).

Disabled People's International (DPI) (1986). 'DPI – Calling', European Regional Newsletter No. 1 (March 1986).

Douglas, M. (1966). *Purity and Danger: An Analysis of the Concepts of Pollution and Taboo* (London: Routledge & Kegan Paul).

Doyal, L. (1979). *The Political Economy of Health* (London: Pluto Press).

Doyal, L. (1983). 'The Crippling Effects of Underdevelopment' in Shirley, O. (ed.).

Edgerton, R. (1967). *The Cloak of Competence: Stigma in the Lives of the Mentally Retarded* (Berkeley and Los Angeles: University of California Press).

Edgerton, R. (1976). *Deviance: A Cross-Cultural Perspective* (London: Benjamin/Cummings).

Elias, N. (1977). *The Civilising Process* (Oxford: Blackwell).

Erlanger, H., and Roth, W. (1985). 'Disability Policy: The Parts and the Whole', *American Behavioural Scientist*, Vol. 28, no. 3.

Estes, C., Swan, J., and Gerard, L. (1982). 'Dominant and Competing Paradigms in Gerontology: Towards a Political Economy of Ageing', *Ageing and Society*, Vol. 2, no. 2.

Evans-Pritchard, E. (1937). *Witchcraft, Oracles and Magic amongst the Azande* (Oxford: Clarendon Press).

Farb, P. (1975). *Word Play: What Happens When People Talk* (New York: Bantam).

Farber, B. (1968). *Mental Retardation: Its Social Context and Social Consequences* (Boston: Houghton Mifflin).

Fiedler, B. (1988). 'Living Options Lottery: Housing and Support Services for People With Severe Physical Disabilities' (London: Prince of Wales' Advisory Group on Disability).

Fiedler, L. (1981). 'Pity and Fear: Images of the Disabled in Literature and the Popular Arts' (New York: International Center for the Disabled).

Finch, J. (1984). 'Community Care: Developing Non-Sexist Alternatives', *Critical Social Policy*, Vol. 9, no. 4.

Fine, M., and Asch, A. (1985). 'Disabled Women: Sexism without the Pedastal' in Deegan and Brooks (eds).

Finkelstein, V. (1980). *Attitudes and Disabled People: Issues for Discussion* (New York: World Rehabilitation Fund).

Finkelstein, V. (1985). Paper given at World Health Organisation Meeting, 24–28 June, Netherlands.

Finkelstein, V. (1987). 'Why Disabled People Need an Arts Organisation', unpublished paper.

Finkelstein, V. (1988). 'Changes in Thinking about Disability', unpublished paper.

Forder, A., Caslin, T., Ponton, T., and Walklate, S. (1984). *Theories of Welfare* (London: Routledge & Kegan Paul).

Foster, G., and Anderson, B. (1978). *Medical Anthropology* (New York: Knopf).

Foucault, M. (1965). *Madness and Civilisation* (London: Tavistock).

Foucault, M. (1972). *The Archeology of Knowledge* (New York: Pantheon).

Foucault, M. (1977). *Discipline and Punish* (Harmondsworth: Penguin).

Foucault, M. (1980). *Power/Knowledge: Selected Interviews and Other Writings 1972–77* (Brighton: Wheatsheaf).

Freidson, E. (1970). *Profession of Medicine: A Study in the Sociology of Applied Knowledge* (New York: Dodd, Mead & Co.).

Fry, E. (1987). 'Disabled People and the 1987 General Election' (London: Spastics Society).

Funk, R. (1987). 'Disability Rights: From Caste to Class in the Context of Civil Rights' in Gartner and Joe (eds).

Gartner, A., and Joe, T. (ed.) (1987). *Images of the Disabled, Disabling Images* (New York: Praeger).

George, V., and Wilding, P. (1976). *Ideology and Social Welfare* (London: Routledge & Kegan Paul).

George, V., and Wilding, P. (1984). *The Impact of Social Policy* (London: Routledge & Kegan Paul).

Gerber, J., and Seligman, M. (eds) (1980). *Human Helplessness, Theory and Applications* (London: Academic Press).

Giddens, A. (1984). *The Constitution of Society* (Cambridge: Polity Press).

Goffman, E. (1961). *Asylums* (New York: Doubleday).

Goffman, E. (1963). *Stigma: Some Notes on the Management of Spoiled Identity* (Harmondsworth: Penguin).

Graham Monteith, W. (1987). *Disability: Faith and Acceptance* (Edinburgh: Saint Andrew's Press).

Gramsci, A. (1971). *Selections from the Prison Notebooks* (London: Lawrence & Wishart).

Gregory, J. (1987). *Sex, Race and the Law: Legislating for Equality* (London: Sage Publications).

Groce, N. (1985). *Everyone Here Spoke Sign Language: Hereditary Deafness on Martha's Vineyard* (London: Harvard University Press).

Gussow, Z., and Tracey, G. (1968). 'The Role of Self-Help Clubs in Adaptation to Chronic Illness and Disability', *Social Science and Medicine*, Vol. 10.

Gwaltney, J. (1970). *The Thrice Shy: Cultural Accommodation to Blindness and Other Disasters in a Mexican Community* (New York and London: Columbia University Press).

Habermas, J. (1971). *Toward a Rational Society* (London: Heinemann).

Hadley, J. (1988). 'The Hard Sell', *New Society*, 1 August 1988.

Hahn, H. (1985). 'Disability Policy and the Problem of Discrimination', *American Behavioural Scientist*, Vol. 28, no. 3.

Hahn, H. (1986). 'Public Support for Rehabilitation Programs: the Analysis of US Disability Policy', *Disability, Handicap and Society*, Vol. 1, no. 2.

Hamilton, P. (1987). 'Editor's Foreword' in Bocock, R.

Hanks, J., and Hanks, L. (1980). 'The Physically Handicapped in Certain Non-Occidental Societies' in Phillips, W. and Rosenberg, J. (eds).

Harbert, W. (1988). 'Dignity and Choice', *Insight* 25 March 1988.

Hardin, B. (1982). *Collective Action* (Baltimore: Johns Hopkins Press).

Hari, M. (1968). Address given on Conductive Education, Conference on the 'Peto' Method (Castle Priory College, Oxford).

Hari, M. (1975). 'The Idea of Learning in Conductive Pedagogy' in K. Akos (ed.) *Scientific Studies on Conductive Pedagogy* (Budapest: Institute for Motor Disorders).

Harris, A. (1971). *Handicapped and Impaired in Great Britain* (London: HMSO).

Hellman, C. (1984). *Culture, Health and Illness* (Bristol: John Wright and Sons).

Higgins, P. (1985). *The Rehabilitation Detectives: Doing Human Service Work* (London: Sage).

Hirst, P., and Woolley, P. (1982). *Social Relations and Human Attributes* (London: Tavistock).

Heumann, J. (1983). quoted in Crewe and Zola (eds).

Hoad, A. (1986). 'The Impact of Transport on the Quality of Life and Lifestyles of Young People with Physical Disabilities' (London: London School of Hygiene and Tropical Medicine).

Humphreys, L. (1972). *Out of the Closets: The Sociology of Homosexual Liberation* (New Jersey: Prentice-Hall).

Hunt, P. (1981). 'Settling Accounts with the Parasite People', *Disability Challenge* 1 (London: UPIAS).

Hutchinson, D., and Tennyson, C. (1986). 'Transition to Adulthood' (London: Further Education Unit).

Ignatieff, M. (1983). 'Total Institutions and the working classes: a review essay', *History Workshop Journal*, 15.

Illich, I. (1973). *Tools for Conviviality* (London: Calder & Boyars).

Illsley, R. (1981). 'Problems of Dependency Groups: The Care of the Elderly, the Handicapped and the Chronically Ill', *Social Science and Medicine* Vol. 15A.

Jones, K., and Tillotson, A. (1965). 'The Adult Population of Epileptic Colonies' (London: British Epilepsy Association and International Bureau for Epilepsy).

Kleinman, A. (1980). *Patients and Healers in the Context of Culture* (London: University of California Press).

Kittrie, N. (1971). *The Right to be Different: Deviance and Enforced Therapy* (Baltimore: Johns Hopkins).

Kumar, K. (1978). *Prophecy and Progress. The Sociology of Industrial and Post-Industrial Society* (Harmondsworth: Penguin).

Kutner, N. (1979). 'Race and Sex as Variables Affecting Reactions to Disability', *Archives of Physical Medicine and Rehabilitation*, Vol. 60, no. 2.

Laclau, E., and Mouffe, C. (1985). *Hegemony and Socialist Strategy. Towards a Radical Democratic Politics* (London: Verso Press).

Ladd, P. (1988). 'Hearing-impaired or British Sign Language Users? Social Policies and the Deaf Community', *Disability, Handicap and Society*, Vol. 3, no. 2.

Le Grand, J. (1978). 'The Distribution of Public Expenditure: the Case of Health Care', *Economica*, Vol. 45.

Le Grand, J., and Robinson, R. (ed.) (1984). *Privatisation and the Welfare State* (London: Allen & Unwin).

Leonard, P. (1984). *Personality and Ideology: Towards a Materialist Understanding of the Individual* (London: Macmillan).

Lévi-Strauss, C. (1977). *The Elementary Structures of Kinship* (London: Beacon Press).

Liggett, H. (1988). 'Stars are Not Born: An Interactive Approach to the Politics of Disability', *Disability, Handicap and Society*, Vol. 3, no. 3.

Longmore, P. (1987). 'Screaming Stereotypes: Images of Disabled People in Television and the Motion Pictures', in Gartner and Joe, (eds).

Lonsdale, S. (1986). *Work and Inequality* (London: Longman).

Lord, G. (1981). *The Arts and Disabilities: A Creative Response to Social Handicap* (Edinburgh: MacDonald).

Lukes, S. (1973). *Individualism* (Oxford: Basil Blackwell).

McCarthy, M. (1986). *Campaigning for the Poor: CPAG and the Politics of Welfare* (Beckenham: Croom Helm).

Manion, M., and Bersani, H. (1987). 'Mental Retardation as a Western Sociological Construct: a cross-cultural analysis' *Disability, Handicap and Society*, Vol. 2, no. 3, pp. 231–46.

Manning, N. (1985). 'Constructing Social Problems' in Manning (ed.).

Manning, N. (ed.) (1985). *Social Problems and Welfare Ideology* (Aldershot: Gower).

Manning, N., and Oliver, M. (1985). 'Madness, Epilepsy and Medicine' in Manning (ed.).

Martin, J., Meltzer, H., and Elliot, D. (1988). *The Prevalence of Disability Amongst Adults* (London: HMSO).

Martin, J., and White, A. (1988). *OPCS Surveys of Disability in Great Britain – Report to: The Financial Circumstances of Disabled Adults Living in Private Households* (London: HMSO).

Marx, K. (1913). *A Contribution to the Critique of Political Economy* (Chicago).

Meacher, M., Beckett, M., and Morris, A. (1986). 'As of Right' (London: House of Commons).

Mead, G. H. (1934). *Mind, Self and Society – from the Standpoint of a Social Behaviourist* (Chicago: University of Chicago Press).

Midwinter, E. (1987). 'Old is not Senile', *The Health Services Journal*, 12 November 1987.

Miller, E., and Gwynne, G. (1972). *A Life Apart* (London: Tavistock).

Moore, J. (1988). *The Independent*, n.d.

Morris, P. (1969). *Put Away* (London: Routledge & Kegan Paul).

Murphy, R. (1987). *The Body Silent* (London: Dent).

Nathwani, A. (1987). 'Disability in the Asian Communities' (London: Greater London Association for Disabled People).

National Council for Voluntary Organisations (NCVO) (1984). 'A Multi-Racial Society: The Role of National Voluntary Organisations' (London: Bedford Square Press).

Navarro, V. (1976). *Medicine under Capitalism* (London: Croom Helm).

NISW (1988). *A Positive Choice* (London: HMSO).

OECD (1987). 'Handicap and Adult Status: Policy Issues and Practical Dilemmas' (Unpublished).

Offe, C. (1980). 'The Separation of Form and Content in Liberal Democratic Politics', *Studies in Political Economy*, Vol. 3.

Oliver, M. (1978). 'Medicine and Technology: Steps in the Wrong Direction', *International Journal of Medical Engineering and Technology*, Vol. 2, no. 3.

Oliver, M. (1979). 'Epilepsy, Self and Society: A Study of Three Groups of Adolescent Epileptics', Ph.D. Thesis, University of Kent.

Oliver, M. (1981). 'Disability, Adjustment and Family Life' in Brechin *et al.*

Oliver, M. (1983). *Social Work with Disabled People* (London: Macmillan).

Oliver, M. (1984). 'The Politics of Disability', *Critical Social Policy*, 11.

Oliver, M. (1985). 'Discrimination, Disability and Social Policy' in Brenton, M., and Jones, C. (eds), *The Yearbook of Social Policy 1984–5* (London: Routledge & Kegan Paul).

Oliver, M. (1986). 'Social Policy and Disability: Some Theoretical Issues', *Disability, Handicap and Society*, Vol. 1, no. 1.

Oliver, M. (1987). 'Re-defining Disability: Some Issues for Research', *Research, Policy and Planning*, 5.

Oliver, M. (1987b). 'From Strength to Strength', *Community Care*, 19 February 1987.

Oliver, M. (1988). 'The Political Context of Educational Decision Making: The Case of Special Needs' in Barton, L. (1988).

Oliver, M., and Hasler, F. (1987). 'Disability and Self-help: A case study of the Spinal Injuries Association', *Disability, Handicap and Society*, Vol. 2 (2), pp. 113–25.

Oliver, M., Zarb, G., Silver, J., Moore, M., and Salisbury, V. (1988). *Walking into Darkness: The Experience of Spinal Injury* (London: Macmillan).

Oyen, E. (ed.) (1986). *Comparing Welfare States and Their Futures* (Aldershot: Gower).

Parker, R. (1988). 'A Historical Background' in Sinclair (ed.).

Pasternak, J. (1981). 'An analysis of social perceptions of epilepsy: increasing rationalisation as seen through the theories of Comte and Weber', *Social Science and Medicine*, Vol. 15E, no. 3.

Quicke, J. (1985). *Disability in Modern Children's Fiction* (London: Croom Helm).

Rasmussen, K. (1908). *People of the Polar North* (Philadelphia: Lippincott).

Reiser, S. (1978). *Medicine and the Rise of Technology* (New York: Cambridge University Press).

Rothman, D. (1971). *The Discovery of the Asylum* (Boston: Little, Brown & Co.).

Royal College of Physicians (1986). 'Physical Disability: 1986 and Beyond' (London: RCP).

Rubin, D., Barnett, C., Arnold, W., Freiberger, R., and Brooks, G. (1965). 'Untreated Congenital Hip Disease', *American Journal of Public Health*, Vol. 55, no. 2.

Ruffini, J. (ed.) (1984). *Advances in Medical Social Science* (London: Gordon and Breach).

Ryan, M. (1988). 'A Last Civil Rights Battle', *Guardian*, 20 July 1988.

Ryan, J., and Thomas, F. (1980). *The Politics of Mental Handicap* (Harmondsworth: Penguin).

Safilios-Rothschild, C. (1970). *The Sociology and Social Psychology of Disability and Rehabilitation* (New York: Random House).

Scott, R. (1969). *The Making of Blind Men* (New York: Russell Sage Foundation).

Scott, R. (1976). quoted in Bynder, H., and Kong-Ming New, P. 'Time for a Change: From Micro-to Macro-Sociological Concepts in Disability Research', *Journal of Health and Social Behaviour*, Vol. 17, pp. 45–52.

Scull, A. (1977). *Decarceration: Community Treatment and The Deviant. A Radical View* (New Jersey: Prentice-Hall).

Shapiro, M. (1981). 'Disability and the Politics of Constitutive Rules' in Albrecht (ed.).

Shearer, A. (1981). *Disability: Whose Handicap* (Oxford: Blackwell).

Shirley, O. (ed.) (1983). *A Cry for Health: Poverty and Disability in the Third World* (Frome: Third World Group and ARHTAG).

Silver, R., and Wortman, C. (1980). 'Coping with Undesirable Life Events' in Gerber, J., and Seligman, M. (eds).

Sinclair, I. (ed.) (1988). *Residential Care: The Research Reviewed* (London: HMSO).

Soder, M. (1984). 'The Mentally Retarded: Ideologies of Care and Surplus Population' in Barton and Tomlinson (1984).

Sokolowska, M., Ostrowska, A., and Titkow, A. (1981). 'Creation and Removal of Disability as a Social Category: The Case of Poland' in Albrecht, G. (1981).

Stafford, M., and Scott, R. (1986). 'Stigma, Deviance and Social Control: Some Conceptual Issues' in Ainley *et al.*

Stone, D. (1985). *The Disabled State* (London: Macmillan).

Susser, M., and Watson, W. (2nd edn) (1971). *Sociology in Medicine* (London: Oxford University Press).

Sutherland, A. (1981). *Disabled We Stand* (London: Souvenir Press).

Szasz, T. (1966). 'Whither Psychiatry' *Social Research*, Vol. 33.

Taylor, D. (1977). *Physical Impairment – Social Handicap* (London: Office of Health Economics).

Taylor, R. (1979). *Medicine Out of Control* (Melbourne: Sun).

Taylor-Gooby, P., and Dale, J. (1981). *Social Theory and Social Welfare* (London: Edward Arnold).

Thomas, W. I. (1966). In Janowitz, M. (ed.), *Organization and Social Personality: Selected Papers* (Chicago: University of Chicago Press).

Thorpe, C., and Toikka, R. (1980). 'Determinants of Racial Differentials in Social Security Disability Benefits', *Review of Black Political Economy*, Vol. 10, no. 4.

Titmuss, R. (1968). *Commitment to Welfare* (London: Allen & Unwin).

Tomlinson, S. (1981). 'The Social Construction of the ESN (M) Child' in Barton and Tomlinson (1981).

Topliss, E. (1979). *Provision for the Disabled*, 2nd edn (Oxford: Blackwell with Martin Robertson).

Topliss, E. (1982). *Social Responses to Handicap* (Harlow: Longman).

Touraine, A. (1981). *The Voice and the Eye: An Analysis of Social Movements* (Cambridge: Cambridge University Press).

Townsend, P. (1979). *Poverty in the United Kingdom* (Harmondsworth: Penguin).

Townsend, P. (1981). 'The Structured Dependency of the Elderly: A Creation of Social Policy in the Twentieth Century', *Ageing and Society*, Vol. 1. no. 1.

Townsend, P. (1986). 'Democracy for the Poor', Foreword in McCarthy.

Trieschmann, R. (1980). *Spinal Cord Injuries* (Oxford: Pergamon Press).

Turner, B. (1984). *The Body and Society* (Oxford: Basil Blackwell).

Turner, B. (1987). *Medical Power and Social Knowledge* (London: Sage).

Turner, V. (1967). *The Forest of Symbols: Aspects of Ndembu Ritual* (New York: Cornell University Press).

UPIAS (1976). 'Fundamental Principles of Disability' (London: Union of the Physically Impaired Against Segregation).

UPIAS (1981). *Disability Challenge*, Vol. 1 (London: UPIAS).

Walker, A. (1980). 'The Social Creation of Poverty and Dependency in Old Age', *Journal of Social Policy*, Vol. 9, no. 1.

Walker, A. (1984). 'The Political Economy of Privatisation' in Le Grand and Robinson.

Warnock Report (1978). *Special Educational Needs* (London: HMSO).

Weale, A. (1988). 'New Social Movements and Political Change', Draft Initiative Proposal prepared for ESRC Society and Politics Research Development Group.

Weber, M. (1948). *The Protestant Ethic and the Spirit of Capitalism* (New York: Free Press).

Weber, M. (1968). *Economy and Society*, 3 vols (New York: Bedminster Press).

Wilding, P. (1982). *Professional Power and Social Welfare* (London: Routledge & Kegan Paul).

Wilkin, D. (1987). 'Conceptual Problems in Dependency Research', *Social Science and Medicine*, Vol. 24, no. 10.

Williams, G. (1983). 'The Movement for Independent Living: An Evaluation and Critique', *Social Science and Medicine*, Vol. 17, no. 15.

Williams, P., and Rosenberg, J. (eds) (1980). *Social Scientists and the Physically Handicapped* (London: Arno Press).

Winkler, F. (1987). 'Consumerism in Health Care: Beyond the Supermarket Model', *Policy & Politics*, Vol. 15, no. 1.

Wood, P., and Badley, N. (1978). 'An Epidemiological Appraisal of Disablement', in Bennett, A. (ed.).

Wood, P. (1981). *International Classification of Impairments, Disabilities and Handicaps* (Geneva: World Health Organisation).

Wright, B. (1960). *Physical Disability: A Psychological Approach* (New York: Harper Row).

Wright Mills, C. (1970). *The Sociological Imagination* (Harmondsworth: Penguin).

Wrong, D. (1970). *Max Weber* (New Jersey: Prentice-Hall).

Zola, I. (1972). 'Medicine as an Institution of Social Control', *Sociological Review*, Vol. 20.

Zola, I. (1979). 'Helping One Another: A Speculative History of the Self-Help Movement', *Archives of Physical Medicine and Rehabilitation*, Vol. 60.

Zola, I. (1981). *Missing Pieces: A Chronicle of Living with a Disability* (Philadelphia: Temple University Press).

Zola, I. (1982). 'Social and Cultural Disincentives to Independent Living', *Archives of Physical Medicine and Rehabilitation*, Vol. 63.

Index